BC   6-20-06

04

THEOLOGY—
THE QUINTESSENCE
OF SCIENCE

THEOLOGY
—THE QUINTESSENCE OF SCIENCE

William B. Turner
B.E.E., M.B.A., D.D. (Hon.)

PHILOSOPHICAL LIBRARY
New York

Copyright 1981 by Philosophical Library, Inc.
200 West 57 Street, New York, N. Y. 10019

All rights reserved

Library of Congress Catalog Card No. 80-82649
ISBN 8022-2375-3

Manufactured in the United States of America

IT IS THE GLORY OF GOD
   TO CONCEAL A THING:
BUT THE HONOUR OF KINGS
   IS TO SEARCH OUT A MATTER.

(The Bible, O.T., Proverbs 25:2)

CONTENTS

I. *CREATION*
1. The Beginning   25
2. The Creation Hymn   35
3. God - BEFORE the Creation of the Universe   46
4. The Creation of the Universe   50
5. The Extensions of Existence   55
6. The First Creation in the Universe   68

II. *DERIVATIONS OF GOD*
7. Initial Creation and the Creation of God   75
8. The Steady-State Existence Concept of God   80
9. The Thinking Process and the Advanced
   Wisdom of God   85
10. Advanced Concept of an Omnipotent God   93

III. *THE SOUL*
11. Concept of the Soul   115
12. The Soul of God   133
13. Heaven - the Repository of God   137

IV. *GOD AND MAN*
14. Main Theological Reason for the Creation
    of the Universe   145

7

15. Other Theological Reasons for the
       Existence of the Universe   156
16. The Relationship of Man to God   163
17. Operational Aspects of Man-Made
       Organizations   168

V. *THEOLOGY AND SCIENCE*

18. Using Theology to Solve Difficult Problems
       in Science   177
19. Derivation of the Speed of Light Using the
       Bible Number   184
20. Theological Determination of the Age and
       Size of the Universe   192

VI. *TERMINATION*

21. Aspects of Eschatology (the End of the Universe)   209
22. God - AFTER the End of the Universe   219

VII. *PERSPECTIVES IN THEOLOGY*

23. Concept of the Repeating Cyclical Universe   227
24. The Happening of Theological Events
       (Why Things Happen)   236
25. Describing God   242
26. The Development of God in the Universe   250
27. Evil   258
28. Love and Hate   276
29. God and Time   286
30. The Next Beginning   292

INDEX (OF SUBJECTS)   297

INDEX OF SCRIPTURES   305

LIST OF ILLUSTRATIONS

Fig. 1 The Tree in Winter   58
Fig. 2 Comparison Block Diagram Showing the
         Major Sections of a Digital Computer
         Alongside the Similar Aspects of the
         Thinking Process   126
Fig. 3 Mathematical Operations Upon the Base "12" 187
Fig. 4 Generalized Curve of Existence   199
Fig. 5 The Beginning of the Steps and Points
         in the Universe   233
Fig. 6 Tabulation of the Development of God   253
Fig. 7 The Mathematical Range of Evil   266
Fig. 8 Tabulation of the First Four Systems
         of the Cosmos   279

CHARTS

Chart 1 Proportions of the Tri-Point Concept   153

PROLOGUE

For those of us who must attempt thinking beyond the immediacy of ourselves, there are many unusual questions that demand answers. For unless there are useful answers, there can be no order or reason anywhere. There can be no room or place for anything. There can be no objects or entities of any kind. There can be no motion or change. In fact, there can be no Universe at all. Therefore, nothing can exist.

Yet our senses seem to perceive that something is there. They act from their base of operations which we call our body. This body acts as a center, and to each of us, it becomes a center of everything. Since something is perceived, our body must be operational. If it operates and experiences effects, it must be said to exist. And if we exist, then we must exist somewhere in something. Therefore, there must be a Universe and it must exist. And, there must be a reason for this existence.

With these brief comments, we begin this presentation in Theology. We shall consider the challenges of Theology as we find them. If there is meaning, we shall deal with that meaning. If there is contradiction, we shall deal with that contradiction. If there is nothing, we shall deal with

11

that nothing. Whatever it takes, we shall deal with it accordingly.

To those of us who want to know, to those of us who should know, and to everyone who feels that there must be knowledge—this book is dedicated.

PREFACE

"Meditate upon these things; give thyself wholly to them: that thy profiting may appear to all."

(The Bible, N.T., 1 Timothy 4:15)

Too long have many mysteries associated with the Universe remained hidden. Too long have numerous concepts with exciting underlying importance been obscured and kept from detailed examination. And, due to this absence of knowledge and intellectual opportunity, some of the most meaningful aspects of Religion have been denied proper perspective and omitted from necessary consideration.

Such has been the situation with Theology. Although it represents one of the most important of all subjects, its capabilities and its usefulness have been given too little attention. Because its subject matter is considered so sacred, it has been elevated to the point where thinking is arbitrarily restricted, thereby summarily preventing any attempts at extended contemplation or additional discussion. Yet since we must deal with our Universe, it becomes absolutely essential that we examine Theology and know something about the hidden facts and the special interpretations that are so very significant.

Actually, the Universe is a far different place than most people could ever begin to imagine. It could be described as a place of illusion, the "Maya" of the Hindus. It is a place in which the five senses can not be relied upon as a basis for any kind of proper interpretation, a situation that has been noted by the ancient Greek philosophers in their "sensible" concept (i.e.—of the senses). Where the senses are inadequate, the intellect must become the major means with which to understand the Universe. Thus it is that organized, directed, and referenced thinking must prevail over everything else.

In seeking such knowledge, it is possible to begin by saying that there is a Universe which exists and which was created by some great special power. It can be said that this power is a God or perhaps a set of Gods. It is to this God or Gods that all Religions direct their attention, their devotion, and their rituals. It is the study of God and His relationship to the Universe that becomes the main purpose of Theology.

For Theology to be really meaningful, it must excel in its intended purpose of providing a useful examination of the concept of God. But how can such an overwhelming task be performed? Is it even possible, let alone practical, for Man to ever begin to understand God?

The approach taken herein uses a combination of advanced concepts obtained and analyzed from the various fields of Science, the major Religions of the world, and the techniques of Formal Problem Solving. Science provides for the technological background. The major Religions provide for description and philosophy through their Scriptures and teachings. But it is through the emphasized use of Formal Problem Solving that specific organization, direction, and meaning is developed. With all this utilized in a composite format, the results of this approach provide for new useful interpretations in Theology.

As this approach is developed, the technical background

14

of each topic is examined and defined in extended scientific detail so that the included aspects may be taken to new heights of understanding. When questions are posed such as

Does God exist? and
Is there a Universe?

we must first come to know what it is that is meant by such terms and concepts as "exist" and "Universe." Indeed, "exist" implies some activity by God which must be precisely defined before we can begin to analyze the question. Furthermore, the "Universe" implies some kind of location or situation in which "existence" takes place. Thus it is necessary to know the exact meaning of the included terminology, especially those words located in the more critical positions of each question, BEFORE we can effectively deal with the associated interpretation.

Authoritative aspects and relationships are developed by asking these Theological questions and then considering them from various viewpoints that are conceived and stated in the official Scriptures of the great Religions of the world. Thus these selected quotations, obtained from the different available religious Scriptures, facilitate and correlate the discussions by introducing and presenting specific formally-described Theological concepts and associated ideas already developed by some of the greatest Sages that the world has ever known.

Perhaps the most important feature herein is the extra amount of detailed specific referencing of the included subject material, which is unique for a book on Theology. Four separate scientific books, also written by this author, were used as the basis upon which to develop the Theological concepts. These books examine PHYSICS, TIME, EXISTENCE, and LIFE and provide for the background necessary for the overall perspective herein. Since these four were originated first, it can be said that this fifth book (on Theology) represents the quintessence of Science and is published as the first in the series.

The subject matter of this book has been divided into the following seven sections:

I. Creation
II. Derivations of God
III. The Soul
IV. God and Man
V. Theology and Science
VI. Termination
VII. Perspectives in Theology

Section I deals with CREATION. The concepts of the Creation of the Universe and of what happened BEFORE this monumental event took place, are examined in detail. Perhaps the most unusual aspect of all this is the question—

What was the very first thing that was
created in the Universe?

The description of this special happening (covered in Chapter 6) is actually based upon and developed from the mathematics derived in the book of EXISTENCE. It was the answer to this particular question that literally cried out for further discussions and then became the major single influencing factor that led to this book on Theology.

Section II presents the DERIVATIONS OF GOD. Four separate referenced derivations of God are developed and examined in highly organized and coordinated discussions. The first two (Initial Creation and the Steady-State Existence Theories) cover the most commonly conceived conceptions of God and His origin. These form the basis from which we

16

move into the next two more advanced concepts. The subtle aspects of the thinking process are examined, along with the thinking requirements and the associated implications that bear upon God and His operating environments. From here, the included discussions provide the determination of the actual capabilities and the powers of God, and how these are manifested. Thus a full description of God is developed from the Religious, the theoretical, and the practical points of view.

Section III deals with THE SOUL. The concept of The Soul is developed and described in unusually complete detail, using Existence Theory, Life Theory, Physics Theory, and Time Theory as the combined references. This special description of the Soul is augmented with mathematics that provide unprecedented depth and accuracy. The unexpected geometry of the Soul will prove to be quite surprising. The resulting inferences are exciting, well beyond anything that has ever been presented before. The effects of health and personality problems are introduced (and continued into the book of LIFE in accordance with their applicable bearing upon the discussions therein).

It is the Soul of God which becomes one of the most advanced concepts in all Theology. It is used to examine the identification of God outside of the realm of Existence, and before the time when the Universe was created. In addition, aspects of the Soul of God are considered with respect to TIME THEORY. Finally, all this is tied together by examining the geometry of Heaven—to determine the location of God.

Section IV examines the relationships of GOD AND MAN. From the purely theoretical, we now move to the more practical aspects of Theology. We examine the questions—

Why did God create the Universe? and
Why does the Universe continue to exist?

When PHYSICS THEORY and EXISTENCE THEORY are used to provide the background and the referencing, the resulting interpretations of these questions become a far more different matter than most people would ever begin to suspect.

One of the most unusual topics is presented in Chapter 17. This is the only non-Theological chapter in the entire book. Provided herein is the psychology and the mechanics of Organizational Theory, which deals with the recruiting and especially the utilization of groups of people to accomplish particular tasks and activities. Chapter 17 describes the characteristics of man-made organizations which are used to facilitate Religion and promote mass faith in God.

Section V considers THEOLOGY AND SCIENCE. This section will come as a distinct surprise to those who have only regarded Theology as just a subject that encourages a faith in God. For Theology offers the unusual capability of dealing with and providing solutions to difficult problems in Science. Although it was Science which provided the referencing for all the previous discussions, now the process is reversed to show how Theology can reference Science. To illustrate this, two very difficult Scientific problems are solved with help from THEOLOGY THEORY and are presented with full mathematical interpretation. This includes the theoretical derivation of the Speed of Light, and the determination of the actual Age of the Universe. Thus Theology takes on a new and important status as a universal subject that encompasses all others.

Section VI deals with TERMINATION. The aspects and the consequences caused by the ending of the Universe are examined using concepts already established within Theology. For the first time in this book, we find some divergence between the interpretations herein and those of the Scriptures of the various Religions. Indeed, prior to this section, there has been considerable correlation of the concepts developed in this book with the major ideas presented by the Scriptures and the teachings of the great Religions of the world. But this is not so here concerning the aspects of the Termination of the Universe. Especially are these implications intriguing in what they infer.

Section VII deals with *PERSPECTIVES IN THEOLOGY*. The possibility of a Repeating Cyclical Universe is presented which forms the prelude to the Concept of Predestination. From this and the mathematics of the Steps and the Points develop the aspects of Free Will and the theory of why things happen. This includes a discussion on patterns of thought and what is involved in determining the happening of events.

The various concepts, including the relationships of the associated Conditions and the Environment already presented throughout the book, are brought together to develop the Theological conclusions. An overall extended perspective of God is compiled with a detailed description and examination. There is a concurrent development of the manifestation of God which directly corresponds to the actual development of the existent Universe.

The subject of Evil is easily the most controversial and the most critical in all of Theology. It is given very special attention and a detailed mathematical treatment. It is revealed to have its own separate domain which is definitely apart from God and His manifestations. It is seen as something that is beyond the control of God. It is shown to have its own set of unique relationships which can bear upon Life and Matter, but NOT upon Energy.

19

After the identification of Evil as a distinct and separate entity, continued examination discloses that Love and Hate also can be isolated to their own separate domains. Love, Hate, Evil, and Good are developed as a composite quaternary whose symbolism goes well beyond all the original interpretations that have often been considered by Theology. An infinite mathematical series is developed which forms the basis of providing the capability to derive a mathematical value (or set of values) for the Deities in any Theological monotheistic or polytheistic system.

Time has its own relationships with God. Since this intricate subject of Time has come up in numerous discussions, aspects of God and Time are reviewed and considered with respect to each other.

With these considerations and with the end of the entire Universe comes a need to evaluate the associated status of God. Within the context of this situation, examination is made into the possibility of the occurrence of another Creation taking place through a new Beginning.

The overall objective of this book has been to stimulate thinking in numerous neglected areas of Theology. Emphasis has been given those areas where all too often the statement has been especially used that the more elusive concepts of Theology must not be questioned but accepted on faith only. If a subject is really that important and useful, then it should easily overcome any test of questions, and be that much the better for them.

Theology is a truly inspiring subject. It is exciting and meaningful, well beyond the arbitrary intellectual boundaries to which it has been unnecessarily limited. Therefore in an effort to make Theology even more appreciated, extra interpretation has been offered by providing new sets of answers. It is the author's purpose to promote additional understanding in Theology, and to provide new intellectual means so that others will be able to take this important area even further.

PRELUDE

COME WITH ME AND WE SHALL BEGIN.
WHAT FOLLOWS SHALL BE A CHALLENGE
  TO THOUGHT AND A REVELATION IN
  COMPREHENSION.
AN AWARENESS SHALL OCCUR, AND WITH IT
  AN INSTANT OF MEANING.
THE MOMENT IS NOW AND THE PLACE IS HERE.
SO COME WITH ME NOW AND ALLOW YOURSELF
  TO CONTEMPLATE BEYOND THE APPARENCY
  OF YOUR SENSES.
FOR UNDERSTANDING AND FULFILLMENT ARE
  WITHIN THE GRASP OF YOUR OWN EFFORTS.

Part I

CREATION

1

THE BEGINNING

*"Hast thou not heard long ago, how I have
done it; and of ancient times, that I have
formed it? now I have brought it to pass,"*
(The Bible, O.T., Isaiah 37:26)

In the Beginning, there came to be a Universe which was
represented by many phenomena. And these manifested
themselves in many ways. As they appeared, they were said
to exist. Out of this existence, they expanded and they inter-
acted. From their original single placements, they were
grouped, organized, and oriented into a variety of arrangements and patterns. Their presence, overwhelming at times,
demanded that they be recognized and examined. It became
mandatory that they be identified and considered from an
overall perspective to provide meaning and understanding.

For in this development from the Beginning, something
was appearing, something not quite fathomable. It was said
that there was a God or perhaps many Gods who were responsible for the something. It was said that the something
was a Universe. This Universe and all in it were said to exist.
And in this existence, it was said that there was meaning.

This something, and everything associated with it, was said
to be phenomena. It was said to be, to manifest itself, to
appear, and most of all to exist.

From out of all this came attempts at interpretation. These were made by the thinking creatures. Especially Man (or the one that thinks) began to question. In his restlessness and ceaseless inquiry, he began to question his surroundings, his existence, his origin, and his destiny. He sought meaning and purpose, and the how and the why of his being.

All around him things happened, and they affected him for better or for worse. As the happenings occurred, he inferred that there were reasons behind them. And if there were reasons, then there was something causing these reasons, something with special purpose and the capability to exercise that purpose.

Thus came the ideas that there were great forces at work in the Universe. Behind these great forces seemed purpose. And behind this purpose was conceivably something of a higher form that was directing everything that was happening or coming into being.

What this higher form of life was could only be attempted and grasped at by the intellect. It was something that the senses could not perceive. It was apparently there, at least somewhere. But where? Could anything provide a suitable answer?

The animals became the first candidates to be considered for this position of a higher life form, for they were alive and they could make their presence most apparent. They were variously frightening, they were gentle, they provided food and clothing. But most of all, they were near. They could be seen. They were sharing the environment with man. They had to have some additional purpose.

The control of everything in the Universe had to be attributed to something. Certainly Man had no such power. Therefore this control had to be with the other forms of life, which were represented by the animals.

But no single animal seemed capable of having more than some particular dominant single power. Upon considering

26

this situation, each type or category of happening was delegated as having been done by a particular animal. Thus all the animals had to be given respect and ultimately veneration.

Eventually, it appeared that all of the unknown phenomena and happenings could not be explained away with just animals. Indeed, the rain, wind, and Sun proved to be powerful entities that needed appeasement and entreaty in themselves. Accordingly, special aspects of life were assigned to these commanding entities, thereby necessitating the creation of Animism.

After a while, it became apparent that the spirits and demons, that had developed from the concept of Animism, could have existences independent of their originally associated entity or object. As the complexity and sophistication of these concept developments increased, full-fledged deities were conceived. With all this coming into being, Man began to grope with the possibility that there were one or perhaps more supreme beings in this emerging pantheon of deities.

With this background, the concept of God had its beginning. This beginning paralleled that of the Universe. So God became identified with the Universe, and all its many happenings became associated with Him.

With God, came the basis for the Religions. These had had their origins in the heritage of the past and many of these ideas and practices were adapted into the rituals and the organization of the new emerging Religions. Indeed, a number of the various practices of the ancient Egyptian Religion with its dominant Sun God Ra or Re, and its more than 2,000 animal gods, became included into some of the aspects and rituals of the Western Religions of Judaism, Christianity, and Islam. Even the word *Religion* is believed to have originated from the name of the followers or choosers of *Re*, the *Re-legion*.

The acceptance of the new major Religions by more and

more people brought about the demand for a greater overall coverage and more detail in the associated Theology. It became obvious that much more information would have to be developed to support the Religions and to provide the numerous required explanations.

But how were these explanations to be handled, let alone provide some measure of depth and detail? How could these concepts be examined? Were answers even possible, or are there some things that can never be explained?

Perhaps it is the Zen Buddhists who have offered some of the best commentary dealing with the attendant problems. Language, any language anywhere in the world, is an imperfect instrument at best. Zen Buddhism believes in actually searching for reality and truth, while a language only symbolizes these concepts. Thus the Zen Buddhist believes that the ultimate concepts can *never* be explained, they can only be experienced. Part of this experience process is considered to be through meditation (zen) and part is considered to be through intuition (prajna). Whatever the actual answers are in the search for the ultimate enlightenment (satori), the intellect will be hard pressed in its efforts to find them.

Taoism, like Zen Buddhism, also believes that experience is such that it must surpass the capabilities of expressed language. The experience of the way (Tao) is the actual power (te). Thus the book "Tao te Ching" (attributed to Lao-tse) offers concepts dealing with the power of the way of change (Ching).

Hinduism, perhaps the oldest of the world's major Religions, offers its own particular set of explanations. These are considered by many to be the most intricate and yet the most complete explanations that are provided by any Religion. There are a profusion of reasons given for almost every conceivable kind of happening. Thus meaning is interpreted from everything. And everything is by the Gods to provide for Pantheism operating through a unique form of Polytheism.

Zoroastrianism offers its explanations in terms of contrast and dualism. By having and considering two extremes, there is a continual interplay of one extreme against the other. Thus answers can be obtained in terms of various combinations of opposing pairs of considerations such as good and evil, light and dark, right and wrong, and even contrasting Gods. The ultimate sources of each set of all these included extremes are considered to repose in the two opposing Gods called Ahura Mazda (Good) and Ahriman (Evil).

It should be noted that all the major Eastern Religions (Hinduism, Buddhism, Confucianism, Shintoism, Zoroastrianism) have aspects of Polytheism. All the major Western Religions (Judaism, Christianity, and Islam) are essentially Monotheistic.

The Western Religions offer explanations that generally reflect what is considered the will of one supreme God. The manifestations of all the phenomena and the operations of the Universe represent the exercising of His will. All explanations begin with this premise. Lacking the Deities representing evil which are noted in the Eastern Religions, the problems of evil are attributed to a Devil (or Satan) who, though very prominent, does not enjoy God-type status. Thus the Western Religions rely upon Monotheism with one God responsible for all things.

Of the three Western Religions, Judaism historically came first. It forms the Theological basis for each of the other two, which offer their own specific variations. Christianity has a human-type representation of its God coming down to Earth in a manner similar to the avatar arrangement of the Hindus. Islam builds upon what went before in Judaism and Christianity but rejects the Christian avatar situation, calling Jesus an apostle of Allah (or God). Instead, Islam believes that

God chose one particular human (Muhammed) to be His spokesman (or Prophet).

During the history of the Earth (and perhaps the Universe), many Religions were started or came into being. After some particular period of time, most of these did not survive. Only a small few of these were able to gain the necessary dominance and characteristic advantages to continue. When they did so, it was claimed that God was on their side which helped maintain and advance their religious position. Whatever the reasons, out of all this emerged the major Religions of the world.

Thus in the beginning, Religion came into the Life of Man. Religion became necessary to Man because it served many functions. It provided answers, order, meaning, and purpose. It gave direction and reasons for the inexplicable happenings in which Man always seemed to be involved. This involvement was terribly difficult for the most part. Life was hard. The environmental dangers were many. Food was often difficult to obtain. Many times it would seem that everything was in collusion in a gigantic conspiracy against Man. The surroundings, the Earth, the forces of nature, and the Powers that controlled them—all appeared to combine against Man.

Therefore, it was to these unseen powers that all attention had to be concentrated. They had to be placated, appeased, understood (at least to some measure of appreciable usefulness), and finally invoked for the attainment of some benefit to Man.

Religion offered the answers, the only answers. Since Man seemed responsible for those things immediately associated with him, surely there were greater powers at work directing and responsible for the greater happenings. Thus Man had to reach out to these powers and ask them to intervene and work on his behalf.

Since knowledge of these higher powers was almost totally lacking, their associated behavioral responses were invoked and observed. Man would offer and try different placating ceremonies. If nature, environment, or circumstances did not respond favorably, the immediately offered placating initiations and ceremonies were revised or discontinued. However, when these attempts seemed to work (at least to the point where there were no immediately attendant detrimental consequences), these attempts were repeated and relegated to the status of formal rituals. These were modified and improved upon until they resulted in an organized operating system that had order and repetition. The further refining of each such "system" led to the natural consequence of that which is called "Religion."

With Religion came a social unification and an order that was greater than any previous type of man-made organizational structure. The included rituals required someone to conduct them. Thus religious leaders came into being as a distinct craft-category to perform the religious rites.

The main support for each Religion came from its followers who not only provided recognition and allegiance but the necessary materialistic contributions as well. Since each particular Religion was considered to be divinely inspired and referenced by the Gods, it demanded mandatory adherence from everyone included within its geographical domain.

Different Religions developed in different geographical locations. Where these overlapped, problems evolved concerning which one would become the most dominant. Each claimed the sanction and the power of the Gods behind it and demanded unswerving loyalty and political control in its realm. Disputed claims of authority resulted in marked conflict and often open warfare. When any such severe confrontation ensued, the winner gained the prestige of victory

31

which tended to substantiate his claim of divine sponsorship. The loser, since he was obviously not supported by the Gods, would usually lose followers and territory as well. In unusually severe conflict situations, one ultimate result was the end of the losing religion. The abandonment by the Gods was the death-knell of any system that could not muster and command its necessary divine support.

Out of all this turmoil, conflict, and confusion, came the emergence of the world's major Religions. Each competed against the others until it achieved a significant dominance that could be maintained. As part of this inherent development, Theology became a necessary requirement. For answers were needed and had to be provided. There had to be origin, history, ritual, meaning, and purpose—all in a well developed order.

As time moved on, the associated Theologies were improved, revised, and expanded to continually deal with many of the answers so vital in referencing, developing, and maintaining the Religion. Various Theologians examined the many problems and tried to provide suitable explainations. But these were not always forthcoming, particularly in certain difficult areas.

There are many questions in Theology that are so very difficult that, for the most part, they are usually not even attempted. Often when they do arise and demand consideration, they are summarily dismissed with the curt statement that there are some things that we are not meant to know. Such questions usually involve various aspects of the following:

1. Is there a God?
2. Is there a Universe?
3. What is meant by God?
4. How did He come into being?

5. From where did God come?
6. Where is God now?
7. Was there a God before the Creation of the Universe?
8. Is God alive?
9. What are His characteristics and capabilities?
10. What are the powers of God?
11. How does God manifest His powers?
12. What is meant by the wisdom of God?
13. What is meant by the Soul?
14. Does God have a Soul?
15. What is the main Theological reason for the creation of the Universe?
16. How does God relate and fit into the workings of the Universe?
17. What is the actual relationship of Man to God?
18. What would happen to the Universe if God should disappear?
19. Is there an end to God?
20. Is there an end to the Universe?
21. Where is the location of Heaven?
22. What are some of the major man-made effects upon Religion?
23. Does man have Free Will, or is everything predetermined?
24. Is the Universe cyclical, and will it repeat itself?
25. Can God be described?
26. Can Theology be used to solve problems in Science?
27. What is the nature of Evil?
28. How does the problem of Evil affect God?
29. What are the effects of Love and Hate?
30. What is symbolized by the Theological Quaternary of "Love, Hate, Evil, and Good"?

It is to these questions that we will direct and concentrate our attention. For these form the basis of Theology. These represent the substance of Religion. It is only through a referenced understanding of these aspects of Theology that Religion can take on deep and useful meaning and purpose.

We shall now begin with an examination of one of the oldest and one of the most unique of all the Scriptures of the world's major Religions. Belonging to the Vedantic Scriptures of Hindism, this is the CREATION HYMN of the Rig Veda (X:129). This selection is especially useful and appropriate at this point because this unusual document officially deals with something of extreme importance in Theology— the Creation and the Beginning of the Universe.

2

CREATION HYMN

(Rig-Veda X:129)

There was neither existence nor non-existence;
There was no place of air nor sky beyond.
In this fathomless expanse, was there water?
What then was there included, and where was it?

There was neither death nor immortality;
There was no light, nor was there day or night.
That breathless Self, breathed by Its own design;
Except for It, there was nothing else besides.

In the beginning, there was darkness hidden in darkness;
All this was unilluminated chaos.
For the existence of That was void and without form;
And was born by the might and warmth of great power.

In That, desire rose in the beginning;
The first seed of mind and spirit.
Devoted sages searching in their heart,
Found the root of existence in the non-existent.

Through That, was the extension of their cutting line.
What then was above it, and what below it?
There were causes and mighty forces,
For up there was energy yonder to the activities' place.

Who really knows? Who can here declare it?
Whence was it born, whence comes this creation?
The gods were later than this creation,
Who knows then from whence it came into being?

This creation, from whence did it come into existence?
Was it made by itself, or was it not.
He who sees all in highest heaven,
Surely He knows—or perhaps He knows it not.

Of all the scriptures of all of the great religions of the world, perhaps the most unique in addressing the question of the creation of the Universe is the "Creation Hymn" of the Vedantic Scriptures of Hinduism. It is from the Rig-Veda and it is estimated to be over 4,000 years old. It represents one of the oldest of the surviving documents of ancient mankind.

The most remarkable aspect of the Creation Hymn is that it is the only religious scripture that attempts to examine the creation of the Universe in a detailed manner. It asks a number of questions that even today could not be answered by any standard available Theology. Indeed, many of the religions would not even dare attempt to deal with such posed concepts.

The three major Western religions (Judaism, Christianity, and Islam) all rely on the Old Testament of the Bible for their concepts of Creation. Here the earliest statement dealing with this subject is—"In the beginning God created the heaven and the earth" (Genesis 1:1). But what was there before this? What went before? Indeed, was there a before?

It is always assumed that there was God before, but is this really so? As one of its questions, the Creation Hymn asks—

WHO REALLY KNOWS?
WHO CAN HERE DECLARE IT?

But put in such a form, this question, or any like it, only begs the issue. Who really knows? The one who can come up with useful answers or the tools and means for implementing such answers can be said to be the one who really knows.

In its opening chapter, the Old Testament of the Holy Bible does provide information on the steps of the creation progress that occurred AFTER the Initial Creation. No information is provided concerning what happened before. The basic ingredients, such as water, were brought in and introduced without any prior referencing.

Similarly to these problems just raised concerning the text of the Genesis, the Creation Hymn is also vague. In setting its scene, the Creation Hymn asks—"In this fathomless (or unknown) expanse, was there water?" But it then asks—"What then was there included, and where was it?" By asking what was there, it brings up the question concerning the substance or Matter. By asking where was it, it begins to deal with concepts of placement or geometry in the Universe.

The opening statement of the Creation Hymn is especially profound. It describes the condition of the Universe prior to its initial creation as—"There was neither existence nor non-existence." It will be noticed that no mention is made of any pre-existence. The implication is that existence came from non-existence. Indeed this is confirmed in a later line which states that the sages "Found the root of existence in the non-existent." In the Western religions, especially Christianity, there has been marked disagreement among many theologians concerning this one single point. There is no clear-cut definitive statement in the Western religious scriptures that deals with this concept. As a result, many prominent theologians are of the opinion that the act of creation required pre-existent material. Others contend oppositely to this. But the Creation Hymn is most explicit on this particular concept. It states that existence came from the non-existent.

With respect to its content, the Creation Hymn can be considered as being divided into three parts. The first part describes the conditions PRIOR to the Creation (Lines 1-10). The second part (Lines 11-20) concerns itself with the That (The Being of Beings) or that which we call God. The third part (Lines 21-28) provides the commentary with a set of unusual questions that will stagger the conventional available concepts of most established Theologies.

The first part of the Creation Hymn presents a list of important items missing before Creation. Heading this list is the absence of existence and non-existence. Other things specifically cited were the absences of air, sky, water, death, immortality, light, day, and night. But there was something there. That something was the breathless Self or God. It is specifically stated that—"Except for It, there was nothing else besides."

The second part of the Creation Hymn discusses aspects of the "That," the Being of Beings. As this section starts out (Line 11), it cites "the existence of That" and describes it as being "void and without form." Next it is stated that the That "was born (or created) by the might and warmth of great power." The first part of the Creation Hymn has already established that the "That" was there before Creation when "there was nothing else besides." The reasons for all things are attributed to the That as the primal fountainhead by the statement—"In That, desire rose in the beginning." Indeed the concepts of thinking and life are also attributed to It by the statement connecting It with—"The first seed of mind and spirit."

It is especially interesting to note that the statement wherein the sages "Found the root of existence in the non-existent" is in the second part of the Creation Hymn which deals with the That. The implication here is that the creation of the That has its origins in the realm of the non-existent. Thus the existence of the That has its referencing founded in and from the non-existent.

From the That, everything else came to be. This is stated (Line 17) by—"Through That, was the extension of their cutting line." Thus everything was extended through and from the That. This included causes, mighty forces, energy, and all activities.

Of the entire Creation Hymn, the commentary and the questions presented in the last eight lines are its most startling characteristic. Especially there are three statements that for over 4,000 years have defied and continue to defy the capabilities of all the Theologies of all the world's major religions. These statements are:

1. The gods were later than this creation.
2. Was it (the Universe) made by itself, or was it not.
3. Surely He knows—or perhaps He knows it not.

Immediately it will be seen that these statements involve and invoke concepts which are actually outside of the realm of Theology. If the gods were later (or came later) than the creation of the Universe, it would mean that they had no part in its making or production. Thus the creation of the Universe would have to have had causes that were other than Theological. This means that we would have to look elsewhere to determine how the Universe was actually created.

The second statement that asks whether the Universe made itself, is particularly unique. Remember that this state-

39

ment is presented in scriptures that are canonical as recognized in the Hindu Religion. Thus it is an authoritative religious document that asks whether a creation was made by itself rather than by the Creator.

This possibility of something making itself is especially thought provoking. Pursuing this approach, it must be prefaced with the notation that that which existed after creation, did not exist before. Therefore, for something to have made itself, requires an additional control or a memory-like operation to facilitate the process. It is this possibility of some type of memory-like operation that offers a most unusual approach to Creation.

It has already been shown in the book of EXISTENCE that for something to be, it must meet the DEFINITION of its own existence. This is a mandatory requirement that must always be taken into account. Thus something is what it is. This concept is also presented in the Holy Bible where it is stated

> And God said unto Moses, I AM THAT I AM: and he said,
> Thus shalt thou say unto the children of Israel,
> I AM hath sent me unto you.
>
> (Exodus 3:14)

The concept of something being a particular entity, is predicated on the associated set of conditions that that something meets the defining characteristics of that particular entity. If other definitive characteristics were met, then that particular subject entity would have to be considered as being something else.

At first, it might seem that the asking of whether the Universe was made by itself, was a possible argument that was against God. Nothing could be farther from the actual truth. Remember that these words are in Scriptures, and valid scriptures always support God and His Theological position. Thus the sages who developed the Creation Hymn must have had a particular purpose in mind when they included this specific question.

Let us consider this further. The first part of the Creation Hymn examined the situation prior to the creation of the Universe. In the eighth line it is stated that—

"Except for It (or God), there was nothing else besides."

Therefore, God was the only thing identified as being prior to the creation of the Universe. But if the Universe had a creation, isn't it possible that That which we call God also had a creation? After all, we are dealing with and analyzing the Creation Hymn. Could not the subject of the Creation Hymn apply to God as well as the Universe? Indeed, as the name implies, the Creation Hymn is involved with the creation of ALL things.

If indeed God Himself had a beginning, then how was His creation brought about? The Sages who originally worked on the Creation Hymn have set the stage for this monumental event. If the creation of the Universe was an autonomous process wherein the Universe actually made itself, then it is an implied possibility by similarity that the origin of God was also a Self-creation.

The third statement lays further groundwork for this possibility. The question now that we must consider is whether such an autonomous process could have been under the KNOWING control of God. Thus the Creation Hymn ends with what is the most startling of all the commentaries—

"Surely He knows—or perhaps He knows it not."

41

Here the thinking process of God is questioned by the Sages. Indeed, if God does not know certain aspects concerning the Initial Creation, then whatever went on and was involved could not have been with the direct and knowing control of God.

In conjunction with the first statement (The gods were later than this creation), the question of a lack of a knowing control by God takes on an additional aspect. If there was insufficient knowing, perhaps the thinking process of God was not developed enough to provide the capability of the knowing control. Then other relationships would have to take precedent. Such operations would have had to be built into the functionings of the Universe to provide for the mandatory requirements of Creation.

When it is said that—"The gods were later than this creation," we are considering that God may have had a creation which came at a later date than that of the Universe. This implication of a delay could mean that God was NOT fully functional after such a creation. From this, it could be inferred that there was a delay in His development so that there was a period of time during which distinct changes took place.

Just as a Life-form undergoes distinct change and development from creation to maturity, it is possible that That which we call God may also undergo some similar period of change. The point here is that if a God is created, He may not necessarily have His full range of powers and capabilities immediately after His creation. If this is so, then when would it be said that God is in full and knowing control? In the circumstance just after His creation, there could be a period of delay. Thus any requirement to identify the Ultimate Being as a full operational omnipotent God, would necessitate such notation as being AFTER an Initial Creation. This possibility offers an insight into the statement in the Creation Hymn which says—

42

"The gods were later than this creation."

Our discussion would not be complete unless we made a more detailed comparison of the Creation Hymn with the opening section of the Old Testament (O.T.) of the Holy Bible, which states

1. In the beginning God created the heaven and the earth.
2. And the earth was without form, and void; and darkness was upon the face of the deep. And the Spirit of God moved upon the face of the waters.
3. And God said, Let there be light: and there was light.
4. And God saw the light, that it was good; and God divided the light from the darkness.
5. And God called the light Day, and the darkness he called Night. And the evening and the morning were the first day.
6. And God said, Let there be a firmament in the midst of the waters, and let it divide the waters from the waters.
7. And God made the firmament, and divided the waters which were under the firmament from the waters which were above the firmament: and it was so.
8. And God called the firmament Heaven. And the evening and the morning were the second day.

(Genesis 1:1-8)

A number of the lines from the Holy Bible show a startling similarity to those in the Creation Hymn. Genesis 1:2 starts off with using the phrase—

"——was without form, and void;"

In the Creation Hymn, Line 11 uses the phrase—

"——was void and without form;"

Genesis 1:2 continues with "and darkness was upon the face of the deep." This concept of darkness is also cited in the Creation Hymn, Line 9, which states—"In the beginning, there was darkness hidden in darkness;". In addition the Creation Hymn mentions its commentary on "the deep" by citing in Line 3 "this fathomless expanse."

Almost immediately, the subject of water is discussed in both sets of Scriptures. In addition, the subjects of day and night are mentioned in both. Light is also mentioned in both.

A pair of contrasting statements is presented in both sets of Scriptures. In Genesis 1:7, the phrases "which were under" and "which were above" appear. In the Creation Hymn, Line 18 states—"What then above it, and what below it."

This number of similar comparisons suggests the possibility that both of these documents may have been created and written down at about the same time in history. In the book of TIME, there is a chapter entitled—"Archeology and the Dating of Prehistoric Events." Here it is presented that things that take place at the same time, even though they may occur at widely separated locations where there was no physical contact between the main included persons, will exhibit a number of similar characteristics in the resulting forms of the produced endeavors (such as writings and art forms). Thus this may be the case with the Creation Hymn and the first part of the Holy Bible.

Both of these documents represent official Scriptures of their respective Religions. Both of these deal with the earliest possible historic situations known or considered in their Religions. While attempting to deal with similar topics, both documents present similar concepts. In so doing, both documents exhibit a number of similar phrases. Therefore, it would appear that there had to be some type of common influence that has affected both these sets of Scriptures. It is quite possible that both of these were written and originated at approximately the same time.

3

GOD–BEFORE THE CREATION OF THE UNIVERSE

"Shall thy wonders be known in the dark?
and thy righteousness in the land of
forgetfulness?"
(The Bible, O.T., Psalms 88:12)

In the Bible, the very first statement is—"In the beginning, God created the heaven and the earth" (Genesis 1:1). This represents the event of Initial Creation. But what was there BEFORE this monumental event? How shall we develop a description of God that deals with His being and functioning prior to the Creation of the Universe?

According to the concept of Initial Creation, there was nothing before the Universe was created. The Universe implies and is synonymous with that which we call "existence." Without the Universe, nothing exists. This situation in which nothing exists can be further described in terms of the Realm of Nothing (or the Realm of Zero).

The Realm of Nothing is one of the most difficult of all concepts to understand. Within this realm, there are none of the usual attributes or characteristics of the existent Uni-

46

verse. There is a most definite contrast between the existent Universe and the non-existent Realm of Nothing. Indeed, they are just about complete opposites of each other. In the hierarchial order of things, the Realm of Nothing was first. Through the event of the Initial Creation, this condition of non-existence was followed by the existent Universe. The Creation Hymn of the Hindu Vedantic scriptures (see Chapter 2 herein for additional discussion) presents this statement—

"Devoted sages searching in their heart,
Found the root of existence in the non-existent."
—(Rig Veda X:129)

Thus it is inferred that existence had its origins in non-existence. Existence came to be out of non-existence. It is this situation of non-existence that forms the Realm of Nothing.

It is in this Realm of Nothing that God was contained before the Creation of Universe. It is in this Realm of Nothing that an understanding of God must begin and be developed. For just as the seeds of creation have their origin in the Realm of Nothing, the seeds of God have a similar heritage.

The origin or seed of God must have an identification in the Realm of Nothing. If we say that God created the existent Universe, then God must have a presence which is traceable prior to this monumental event. The only thing available prior to this Initial Creation is the Realm of Nothing. Therefore, the presence of God is traceable to the Realm of Nothing.

But the Realm of Nothing is totally different from the existent Universe. Within this Realm, the presence of God does not have the freedom nor the capability to properly function. In this aspect, this origin of God can be compared with a seed. By itself, a seed can not function. It requires coordinating and supporting conditions. However, in the

Realm of Nothing, there is no possibility of any supporting conditions. Therefore, God in the Realm of Nothing must lie dormant except for one capability.

The particular capability of God, which can function in the Realm of Nothing, is the power to initiate or start a happening. This ability (of starting or stopping an operation) is also the characteristic attribute of the concept known as "Time." Thus the concept of God and the concept of Time are identified as having a common aspect in the Realm of Nothing.

Beside this common aspect of God and Time, there is nothing else in the Realm of Nothing. With nothing else in attendance, operating, or in a correlating condition capacity, some very important conclusions can now be drawn. These include:

1. The Realm of Nothing represents a stable continuing steady-state condition of non-existence which is in direct contrast to the changing transitory dynamic condition of the existent Universe.

2. The Realm of Nothing precedes the existent Universe.

3. The existent Universe requires the referencing of the Realm of Nothing (but not vice versa).

4. There is an identification of God in the Realm of Nothing.

5. God has the power to INITIATE and to TERMINATE any event, operation, or happening.

6. The concept of Time actually involves only two intrinsic capabilities which are to INITIATE and to TERMINATE (see the book of TIME).

7. Within the Realm of Nothing prior to the creation of any portion of an existent Universe, the identifiable aspect of God is associated with the concept of Time.

8. Since there is nothing in the Realm of Nothing, there is nothing to Terminate.

9. Of the two possible powers, only the capability to initiate can be used in the Realm of Nothing.

10. The capability to initiate can allow for the origination or beginning of the creation of the Universe.

11. Since there are no operations that can be processed, there can be no functioning of God in the Realm of Nothing.

12. For the most part, the aspect of God in the Realm of Nothing will be dormant.

13. Although there is identification, there is actually no existence of God in the Realm of Nothing.

14. For God or anything else to exist, the necessary conditions for existence must be available.

15. The conditions for existence can not ever apply in the Realm of Nothing.

16. By definition, the conditions for existence are only available and applicable in the existent Universe.

17. Therefore for God to be and to function, it is necessary that there be an existent Universe. Accordingly, it is a mandatory Theological requirement that there be a creation of a Universe.

4

THE CREATION OF THE UNIVERSE

"It is He Who hath created everything
All things that are on earth;
His design understood the Universe
For He gave order and perfection
To the seven firmaments."
(The Koran, S. II. 29)

The various Religions of the world describe the creation of the Universe in a variety of different ways. The first statement in the Bible says—"In the beginning God created the heaven and the earth" (Genesis 1:1). No other details are given. No other clarifications are even attempted. Yet the simplicity of this presentation is subscribed to by the three major western Religions of Judaism, Christianity, and Islam.

Some of the other Religions present much more complex interpretations of this momentous event of Creation. Indeed the eastern Religions of Hinduism and Shintoism have developed quite expressive relationships that offer extensive detail. Others such as Zoroastrianism and Manicheism present contrasting interactions between opposing Gods in especially unique versions of the Creation of the Universe.

50

No matter what explanations are offered, the final result is the Universe itself. For the Universe represents the culmination of the directed efforts of the God or Gods of the various Religious systems. Thus it is that the different systems of Religion deal with and produce a Universe which is a Theological derivation of their own making and which is called out in their own individual terms.

Since we are dealing with the subject of Theology, it is important to realize that, from the Theological point of view, the purpose of the Creation of the Universe must be primarily to meet and serve the needs of God. Since in Theology it is said that God created the Universe, then this Creation represents an act for His own purpose involving some gainful reason associated with Him.

The event of the Creation of the Universe is a happening of monumental importance. It represents a beginning of everything except God. For God is the Creator and is responsible for the Creation.

But the mechanics and the details of the Creation are difficult and most elusive. Indeed this and the lack of knowledge cause most Religions to by-pass the overall concept of the Creation in its entirety. Yet this topic is of especial importance since it will reference and effect everything that will follow in Theology.

The act of creation involves certain definite basic relationships which must always be included and considered when dealing with any part of the associated process. When anything is created, the event results in a something new which was not so before. It can be said that that which results is completely different from that which was before.

For an Initial Creation, the result is the existent realm of the Universe. The contrast of this is what was so before the Creation. If the result is the existence realm of the Universe, the contrast is the prior situation of the non-existent Realm

51

of Nothing. Accordingly, it can be seen that the basis of Creation involves "—the root of existence in the non-existent" (see the Creation Hymn of the Rig Veda in Chapter 2 herein). (See also the book of EXISTENCE.)

The process of Creation thus has its origins in the Realm of Nothing. Within this Realm of Nothing prior to the Creation of the Universe, the presence of God can be identified (see Chapter 3 herein). Of the ONLY two sets of powers attributable to God—Initiation and Termination (see Chapter 10 herein), Initiation is used to begin the operational process of the Initial Creation.

The very first thing created in the existent Universe is the extension of God from the Realm of Nothing (see Chapter 6 herein). Once an existent presence of God is established, then the phenomenon of all further activities of Creation, as well as the functioning of the operations of the Universe, can proceed through this manifestation of God in the existent Universe.

From the critical vantage point established by the first thing (the manifestation of the phenomenon of God) which is created in the Universe, all other creation proceeds. Concurrent with these activities, the capability for geometrical displacement is established through the creation of the container or dimensions of the Universe. These dimensions provide the geometrical means to contain that which is created. These geometrical dimensions represent a primary requirement for Creation. For without the container, there could be no Universe.

Prior to the moment of Creation, there were no geometrical dimensions of any kind. There was just the Realm of Nothing. Within and outside of this Realm of Nothing, there was nothing by definition. This definition also extends to and includes the concept of dimension. Thus there was no existent container before the moment of Creation. When the Initial Creation began, it was mandatory that a container be also established to hold all the various products of that Creation.

Of all the things created and established in the Universe, the most significant in terms of size and amount is the container itself. That which is created and said to exist must first be contained within a common structure involving itself. Then this structure must be placed within an overall encompassing larger structural container system which is represented by the concept of multi-dimensions in the Universe.

With the Creation of the Universe comes the concurrent requirement for the creation of the associated container. As the existent Universe continues to develop, the container must also continue to develop so that it can hold all the increasing existence. Since this container is represented by the multi-dimensions, more and more dimensions become needed to facilitate the process. The resulting effect of this continuing series of multi-dimensions is like producing containers within containers within containers in a never ending sequence. This leads to the consequence of an almost infinite number of dimensions actually being developed in the Universe.

As this development process continues, the existence of the substance of the Universe becomes more and more complex. Each entity has its existence extended into a number of adjacent groups of dimensions. Each entity can be described as having a totality of existence which is distributed among the various dimensions. The greatest amount of this will be located in the highest order or the last dimension created that still contains portions of the entity. The resulting distribution of existence is such that only particular proportions of the whole entity will be in each dimensional group (or container) at any given instant of time. For each separate entity, there will be a distribution relationship that will form a specific pattern that is unique to that entity.

Thus it is that the process begun by the Initial Creation

first manifests an extention of God and then continues to establish the rest of an existent Universe. This process develops through an infinity of dimensions in which the respective portions of the various existences are established and distributed. This extention of existence will continue until the Universe is completed.

5

THE EXTENSIONS OF EXISTENCE

*"This is part of all
Of the things unseen
Which We reveal unto you
By Inspiration."*
(The Koran, S. III. 44)

The concept of existence is fundamental to the Universe. For if the Universe is, it must be said to exist. And in the various aspects associated with existence, each and everything in the Universe can come into being.

The very act of existence implies that that existence must be somewhere. Existence must be contained. The containing of existence infers geometry and dimensions. When existence is considered with respect to geometric dimensions, the being of the existence can be said to extend from some central or reference point on into the associated container.

The Universe can be described as being multi-dimensional (see the book of EXISTENCE). As such, there is almost no end to the possible numbers of these dimensions. If existence by virtue of its included shape, can extend into one dimension, then it is conceivable that it could extend into many

55

more. We shall now look into this possibility of multiple extensions of existence.

From all the approach areas that we might select, it is most fitting that we should begin with *Religion*. For Religion provides the oldest known support for this concept in its general definition of Life. Almost all Religions interpret Life in terms of consisting of two parts. The first is the physical body. This is contained within a volume surrounded by observed apparent specific boundaries whose overall form provides for the outside appearance and the immediate presence of the included individual.

The second part is variously called the life force, spirit, or soul depending on the particular religion. Of special note, *the second part of life is always defined as something other than and apart from the physical.* Thus it can be said that Religion interprets life in terms of two parts where each is separate and apart from the other.

Now let us consider some aspects of each part in more detail. The first part, which is by definition the physical presence, manifests itself by occupying conventional three-dimensional space. The second part, which by definition must be something separate and apart from the physical, must be located somewhere else. That somewhere else, being apart from the physical, implies some location outside and away from the physical. By being away or outside the physical, the implication is that the second part of life as defined by the religious approach, must lie outside conventional three-dimensional space—and therefore must be in another dimension.

Thus from the Religious point of view, life consists of two parts which must operate together with some type of interrelationship. This gives rise to the possibility of operations between multidimensions with something extending between them to provide for coordination and correlation.

Botany, the science dealing with plant life, offers a special area for examining the concepts of existence. A plant is a continuing operation whose objective is to maintain and ultimately perpetuate itself. By this very nature, plants always try to extend their existence. Plant life processes indicate continual extensions in growth and purpose. But there is something more, something that is usually overlooked in most plant operations.

Plants function and operate between two separate and distinct media. In the extremes of their physical environment, most plants exist simultaneously in two separate locations with extensions between to provide for organized operations. The deciduous type of tree provides a specific example.

A tree grows and exists in the Earth and in the sky at the same time. Functions are performed within both places that aid and complement each other. In fact, this duality of existence is a prime necessity for plant operation.

A deciduous tree was chosen as an example for a particular reason. In the Winter time when the tree has lost its leaves, the branches stand out stark and bare. These branches reach out into the sky. Simultaneously, the roots of the tree are in a pattern spread into the Earth. If the pattern of the roots could be viewed, it would be noted that it is very similar to the overall pattern formed by the branches. Thus there is a distinct similarity in the patterns of existence of the tree in its two separate locations or places of existence. To make this point even clearer, a diagram entitled "The Tree in Winter" is presented in Figure 1. The tree is drawn so that both the root and the branch structures are shown. The Earth line is deliberately placed crossing through and dividing the tree trunk in half. The reason for selecting a deciduous tree in winter as an illustrative example should now be clear. During this time, the roots and the branches both exhibit a similar structural pattern. If we turn and view Figure 1 upside down, we still get the same approximate picture.

The branches of a tree are the roots in air while the roots

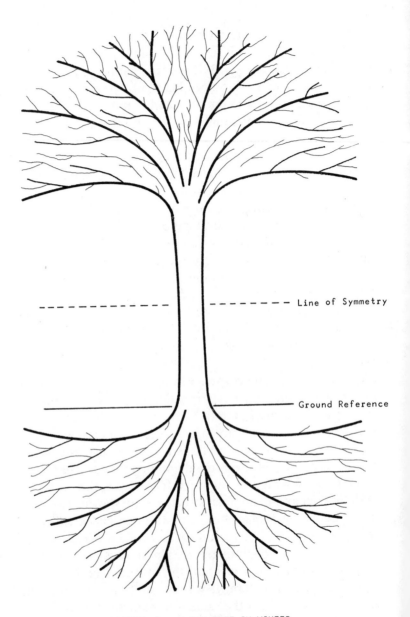

Line of Symmetry

Ground Reference

FIGURE 1 - THE TREE IN WINTER

58

can be considered as the branches in the Earth. Thus it can be realized that plant life operates and exists in two separate and distinct places or media at the same time. The branch and root structures provide the means to allow for extending operations and existence between these two media.

In the field of *Optics,* let us consider the formation and existence of optical images. Typically, optical systems consist of refraction and reflection devices either used singly or on some multiple basis or in some combination. Optics usually deal with a duality known as the object and the image. Each has a definite relationship with respect to the other that depends upon the intervening or included optics. In the optical situation, existence is manifested by the object and image duality while the included optics provide for the means for the extension from one to the other.

In their extension of the object, the optics produce and provide an unusual characteristic for the image. The object usually is considered as something real and existing in proper relation to other physical things. But the image, which is nothing more than an optical projection or extension of the object, is anything but real. It has no direct connection or interpretation with anything that we would usually consider as real. The optical image of food can not be eaten. The optical image of clothing can not be worn. Thus we must conclude that the optical image of a real object has no actual physical reality of its own.

Again we are faced with a duality situation involving something real and something which is related and yet does not fit the general concept of reality. This second something has some kind of existence which is apart from the physical. Look at a mirror and you will see an image of yourself. You will appear to be behind the mirror. The science of physics states that your image will appear as far behind the mirror as you (the physical object) are in front of it. Yet where actually is the image? Physically, it can not be behind the mirror. But,

59

it appears to be there. This effect is sometimes called an illusion or an optical illusion. No matter what it is called or how it is described, the image in the mirror has no physical identity of its own. All we can really say is that it is related to something that is considered real, but it is something else— something apart from reality or the physical.

Let us now combine some *Ophthalmology* with general optics to consider the previous discussion even further. The optical image viewed in the mirror needs an eye for detection. It is the eye that "sees" the image and provides the first step in giving meaning to the image. Now that the process of vision has been initiated, let us take it to its conclusion. A very critical question must be asked. Where is the final image presented to the individual? In other words, where does the final picture of the image actually appear? This seemingly innocuous question currently has no accepted answer. If the question was pressed, a general answer would be that the termination of the process of vision would lie "somewhere" within the brain. When this situation is examined more closely, there is an implication of the possibility of an operation and an associated existence extending beyond conventional 3-dimensional reality.

When an individual performs the act of "seeing," a process takes place that involves the transfer of something between two separate points or locations. The eye provides the input (or optical detection) for this process which is continued via the optic nerves to the brain. The familiar end result is the development of a relatively large picture which could be described as being somewhat similar to that projected upon a screen by a motion picture projector. But where is the counterpart of this "screen" in the brain?

There is a further condition relating to this question that must be explored. What is the size or the ratio of the produced picture in relation to the size of the viewed physical object? In Optics, the ratio of image size to object size is usually called magnification. The most common reference ratio is one-to-one where the image is the same apparent size as the object. (This unity ratio has the convenience of having the magnification being unity so that any variations in the optical system can be discussed as moving away in relative terms from unity.) All flat (or plane) mirrors produce this one-to-one ratio or full-size presentation.

This one-to-one reference ratio is especially important to the functioning of the human vision process. The final picture that the eye sees,will represent a physical size or field of view coverage that is approximately three (3) times the width of the average human head at the one-to-one ratio. Under this condition, the final viewing "screen" could not be contained within the physical volume of the human brain. Therefore, if we do see things "full size," then the final brain image or picture would have to be developed outside beyond the physical volume of the human brain. Again, this would imply the existence of something else away and apart from the physical to accommodate this extended or oversize situation. The implication is the existence of another dimension (or dimensions) in addition to the conventional 3-dimensional space of Euclidean geometry. A further inference is that portions of the human brain and its operations lie in and take place in this other dimension.

Energy, as a general category, is a subject that offers some special ideas on the extensions of existence. Energy is one of the most important basic concepts of the major group of Physics which also includes mass, time, life, thought, etc. Although all these words are used very readily and much too easily, none have a precise indisputable scientific definition. However, by careful organization and usage, some special aspects of Energy can be examined.

When it is discussed, Energy is often considered in terms of where it comes from and where it goes to. Energy can be said to appear at or operate from some initial reference point or location. It can be said to operate upon, be used, or be somehow absorbed at some different other location. Thus when Energy and its effects are discussed, its associated existence is usually considered with respect to at least two different geometric points.

Energy has the intrinsic characteristic to be able to reach out and influence things at a location apart and away from its reference point of origination. Energy has this capability to extend itself away from its existence origin and produce effects at a remote location. Whatever mechanism may cause Energy to function as it does, Energy can somehow extend itself to span and operate between two or more geometric points.

Thus a radio transmitter transmits, a flashlight emits light, a loudspeaker sends out sound, and the Sun sends out heat. Whenever there is Energy then something can be sent out. Therefore, if there is any Energy associated with human brain operations, then the possibility exists that the brain could become the origin point from which something could be sent out. More specifically, if thought and other brain associated processes involve energy then it is conceivable that something could be sent out under the right conditions to influence or cause effects at particular points and locations outside and away from the brain.

In *Biology*, it is believed that the brain is the center for all activity and control in the body. Since activity and control involves Energy, the brain would also be the center of the greatest concentration of Energy in the body. This is backed up in Biology by studies that have indicated that thinking requires the use of more Energy than any other body activity. Thus it would be concluded that the highest concentration of Energy in the human body would be located at the center of thinking during times of heavy thought activity.

Studies of the brain include the general area of *Physiology*. In line with our previous discussions, let us examine concepts

62

dealing with the brain by considering the geometric relation that involves at least two separate points. One very important point is the center of thinking.

For geometric reference purposes, it is very useful to have something which denotes a center of activity or system origin. In studying the brain, an appropriate center is the Center of Thinking. This can be defined as that point from which all thinking can be said to originate. Whatever the mechanism involved in the process of thinking, developed thought will emanate away from this point.

Continuing this approach and assuming there is such a point, exactly where would this Center of Thinking be located? By definition, thought originates at and emanates from this point. For something to come out of a point, something must go in. If it is "thought" that comes out as an originating function (something that is considered to be created at a reference), then what is it that goes in? For example, light originates and emanates from a wire filament in an incandescent lamp. But in the process light only comes from the lamp, it does not enter. Something else enters. In this case, electricity is sent in and light results and is sent out.

If by definition, thought is created and originates at the point Center of Thinking, then something other than thought was sent in. This implies that something else must reference the producing or creating of thought. Thus thinking is not referenced by thought. In our previous example discussing the creation of light in an incandescent lamp, light was described as coming out while electricity was going in. Both the output and input involved different types of energies. It would appear (as referenced by the previous Energy discussion) that "thought" must include some type of energy. In addition, whatever is going into the Center of Thinking must also be some form of energy.

For two energies present at a particular point, the special concept of inter-reaction must be noted. For two things to

63

react at a common point with each other, they can only do so if a common medium is present. The common medium is the key to the interaction. As an example, let us consider the two energies of light and electricity and see how they can be made to have a common reaction. Light can travel in glass, but electricity cannot since glass is an electrical insulator. Electricity can travel in a metallic wire, but light can not since a wire is usually opaque to light. Thus there could be no interaction of light and electricity in either regular glass or metallic wire. However, if a material such as "doped" silicon which is used as an ingredient of transistors was selected, it would be found that both a certain amount of light and electricity can flow or travel in doped silicon (pure silicon into which very small quantities of select chemicals are introduced). In this situation, there would be an interaction. In fact, doped silicon is used to make opto-electrical devices such as photo-diodes and photo-transistors.

The concept of reaction of two things in a common medium can be applied to the operation of the brain at the Center of Thinking. It was previously stated that, by definition, thought was coming out of the Center of Thinking. It was also stated that energy was coming out of the Center of Thinking and that this energy was somehow tied in with the thought. In addition, some other form of energy was going into this reference point. Thus thought is the result or the product of two things, and the brain (or at least some part of it) represents the common medium.

Up to now, the whole discussion presented herein has been intended to relate the geometric concept of two points with some kind of extension between them. Now this concept is going to be further applied to the Center of Thinking of the brain. So far, this discussion of the Center of Thinking has been confined to just one point. But it has been suggested that there is a duality that usually comes into play. Thus it is considered that the Center of Thinking has its counter-part

64

with some type of extension mechanism in operation between these two points.

In *Astronomy*, a star as a source of energy, offers an unusual situation for study. A star is a macro-object and its energy output is huge with respect to its size. To consider it in geometric relation to our previous concepts, a star can be scaled down so that it can be considered as a point source. As such, it would represent a reference point from which energy was emanating. In the scaling down function, the energy output would be scaled down as well as the size. Even though the size was reduced, it would be found that the relative energy output would still be very large as compared to the approaching point size of the star. Again, the summation of activity around a point must be zero. Therefore, the principle of something going in for something coming out would have to be invoked.

We have been dealing with the geometry of points and examining activity in proximity around these points. For such a large output, there must be a large corresponding input activity. But if something is going into a star, WHERE IS IT GOING IN? The Sun is a star whose closeness to the Earth has made it an ideal celestial object for observation and measurement. Yet nothing of consequence has ever been seen to enter the sun.

Again, the main concept previously posed is incurred. Something must go in. If this operation can not be observed in our conventional 3-dimensional space, then it must take place somewhere else. That somewhere must be in another dimension or media. Since the overall relation of "going in—coming out" is involved, then in addition to the extra or multi-dimensions, there must be some means to span or extend between them to permit the full required operations. Thus the existence of a star involved at least two points each in a separate dimensional media or plane of existence with some extensions in-between.

65

Perhaps here, a further example representing a complete contrast would prove useful. From the macro-conditions of a star, consider the micro-aspects of an atom. Let us examine the geometry involved in some operations of *Atomic Energy*, since this is sometimes used as an explanation of the origin of energy in the Sun. An important question to ask is where within the structure of the atom does the atomic energy develop? Is there a point or reference center within the atom that can be used to identify exactly where the resulting energy occurs? For this purpose, the atom can be divided into two zones separated by the outer boundaries of the nucleus. Examinations can be made of locations in each of these two zones.

If a point outside the nucleus is considered, there could be nothing physical to reference that point. If energy was produced in accordance with splitting the nucleus, then theory would place the point inside the nucleus region where it would have to be located within the gap of the split nucleus. Again there would be nothing physical to reference this point. In either case, the placement of the point could not be referenced with any part of the physical or real part of the structure of the atom. Thus there would be relatively large amounts of energy originating or happening from non-physical parts of the atom. The production of atomic energy has geometric aspects that imply an extra-dimensional relationship.

All of the foregoing discussions have implied that operations are happening outside of the regular physical portions of the cited objects. In each instance, an important something related to the object was not occurring or directly associated with the reference object. It appeared that the included effects were happening apart from the regular geometry of the object.

These implications support the possibility that there are extensions to existence. These extensions imply that there are additional geometric dimensions rather than just the conventional three dimensions that we take so much for granted. Indeed, when multi-dimensional theory is considered, the explanations for these happenings take on new and significant meaning. Thus existence involves much more than its immediate apparency would indicate. It has extensions into other groups or tiers of dimensions in addition to the usual three that are commonly considered. The maintenance of existence is actually dependent upon interchanges between these dimensional groups. Therefore, what is considered existence, is some kind of distribution between two or more groups of dimensions with active relationships occurring among this subsequent set of individual distributions.

6

THE FIRST CREATION IN THE UNIVERSE

"——who is the beginning, the firstborn from the dead; that in all things he might have the preeminence."
(The Bible, N.T., Colossians 1:18)

Considering the possibility of an Initial Creation, the question that must accordingly be asked is—What was the first thing that was created in the Universe?

The concept that will be examined now is that after an Initial Creation (which refers to the event that allowed for the origination of the Universe to come out of the initial condition of total nothing or non-existence), the first thing developed in the Universe is a special form of Life. This form of Life has such unique qualities and characteristics that it is going to be compared and identified with That which we describe as being God. The scientific background of the included considerations has already been researched and the results appear in other of the concurrent books of this series.

The existent Universe has been derived in precise mathematical terms in the book of EXISTENCE. Here it has been shown that the very first mathematical representation in the associated series function has a value of exactly 3/4. It is this particular value that is identified with the first something in the Universe.

In summarizing concepts of existence in the Universe, it can be stated that all associated mathematical values must lie between the extreme limits of nothing (0) and the whole (1). In general Existence Theory, there can't be anything less than nothing nor can anything be greater than the whole. Thus all the representative mathematical values of existence will range from 0 to 1 where they can be expressed in decimal or fractional form. Of all the possible values from zero to one, 3/4 occupies a key position both from the geometrical as well as the mathematical point of view. Especially in Multi-Dimensional Theory, it is the only value that can have a uniform extension of itself in every possible dimension (going from one through to infinity) in the Universe. The sum total of all the separate values of each portion of the associated existence that is distributed in prescribed mathematical relationship in each geometrical dimension for the function f(3/4), is exactly one (1). This function is the only one that can have representation and manifest influence in every dimension. It is also the first function that is developed in Existence Theory. Thus it is this fraction of 3/4 that appears first after an Initial Creation and occupies a very special place in the mathematical hierarchy of existence values.

Three mathematical models of the fundamental concepts of existence are specially developed and tabulated in the book of EXISTENCE. These provide numerical representations of the three basic entities of Energy (E), Life (L), and Matter (M). These developed E-L-M Tabulations show the totality and the extent of the specific mathematical values and the included ranges that are associated with each of these three basic entities. The major importance of these E-

L-M Tabulations is that they mathematically represent Energy, Life, and Matter. Therefore, the results of specific mathematical derivations can be compared to these E-L-M Tabulations and then identified in terms of the particular E, L, or M category and the associated relative placement within the identified range.

With respect to the first something in the Universe, its derived value of 3/4 identifies it as being a form of Life, since it falls into the mathematical range of the L-Tabulation. This means of identification is most precise. The L-Tabulation is an independent development relating to Existence Theory. The origination of the 3/4 term is a separate evaluation referenced by the special initial conditions of the Initial Creation. Thus through these independent scientific means, the first something in the Universe is positively identified as being a form of Life.

The concept that the first something in the Universe is a form of Life is especially significant to the field of Theology. Let us consider this form of Life within its general context. As the original entity in the Universe, this Life exists totally by itself at first. There is nothing else. This means that there is no air, no water, no food, no energy nor temperature, and no place for its being. Yet this Life exists. Since it exists and continues to do so without any conventional support nor destructive influences, this Life fits the definition of being IMMORTAL.

From an existence point of view, this Life occupies a very critical position in the Universe. This Life is geometrically located at the most crucial placement and must continue to remain at this decisive pivotal point. Everything else must stem or be traceable to this one key location. This key point is required as an initial condition for everything else in the Universe. Should this point ever disappear with its contents, then everything else in the Universe must become untenable, thereby ultimately resulting in the destruction of the entire

remaining existent Universe. Thus the existence of everything in the Universe is dependent upon the continuing existence of this critical initial Life point.

All the foregoing descriptions represent the Physics and
the associated science relating to this first something in the
Universe. From a Theological point of view, there are a
number of special implications which we must now examine.
For consideration purposes, these implications can be better
seen if we itemize and tabulate what we now have. It will be
noted that everything on this special list represents the very
same thing.

ASPECTS OF THE FIRST THING IN THE UNIVERSE

1. It is a form of Life.
2. It is immortal.
3. It is not subject to the conventional needs of life
(no air, no water, no food, nor anything else).
4. It is situated at the most critical geometrical location in the Universe.
5. It is the fountainhead for everything else.
6. The creation of everything in the Universe must
come and pass through this point.
7. This point must be or there will be nothing else.
8. If this point and its contents should somehow be
destroyed after the Universe (or some portion of it) has
come into being, then the direct result would be that the
entire existent Universe would collapse and ultimately
cease to be.

The major implication of this First Something in the Universe is that it corresponds in a number of aspects to a definition of God. Indeed, a picture begins to emerge that deals
with the main entity of Theology which is God, Himself.

From a Theological point of view, God would have had to

71

be the very first something in the Universe. This first something would have had to be the existent manifestation of God extended from His identification within the non-existent Realm of Nothing (or Zero). The presence of God in the existent Universe would have to be established prior to anything else in the Universe. Then and only then could all the other operations and happenings occur.

Everything else would have had to come after Him and through Him. Certainly, He must occupy the most critical geometrical location in the Universe. In addition, God must be alive, immortal, and must be independent of most conventional needs. For a Universe to come into being and exist, God must exist first as a necessary initial condition, and must continue to exist. If for some inexplicable reason God should cease to exist, it would be expected that the entire Universe would cease to be, regardless of its state of development.

Therefore, for the situation involving an Initial Creation of the Universe, God is considered to be the First Something that is actually created in the total series of associated events and happenings.

Part II

DERIVATIONS OF GOD

7

INITIAL CREATION AND THE CREATION OF GOD

"Greatest of all is Purusha,
All mortals are 1/4 of him,
3/4 eternal life in heaven.
With 3/4 Purusha was there,
1/4 of him was here."
(Hindu, Rig Veda, Hymn of Man, X:90)

One of the greatest challenges to thought is to attempt an understanding of the existence of God. So difficult is this concept that many of the major religions have bypassed this area completely. Indeed, the Bible, which forms the basis of three of the world's major religions, starts with "In the beginning God created the heaven and the earth." (Genesis 1:1.) Yet no attempt is made to go before this point in time. All that can be done is to assume that God existed prior to this creation in the Universe. But what about this existence? If the Universe was created where it did not exist before, is it possible that God also had an initial creation? In such an investigation, there can be many possibilities. In the following chapters, we shall examine three other categories that consider different approaches and offer other answers. Right now, we shall explore the possibility that God was the subject of an Initial Creation.

Prior to discussing God, the concept of what is meant by an initial creation must be examined and understood to provide a sufficiency of background. A creation means that something is generated. But the word "initial" is a special modifier that implies a "first operation." A first operation means that there was nothing similar prior to this before. In this case, we are dealing with the most special condition of them all. This involves *the* Initial Creation of and in the Universe.

When we speak of *the* Initial Creation in the Universe, the condition is implied that a state of total nothing was in effect prior to this first operation. This means that there was no pre-existent material nor anything else. It should be noted that there absolutely were no dimensions or place to put a something, which is a further condition of a total nothing. The creation of dimension and ultimately the multi-dimensions in the Universe is discussed in the book of EXISTENCE. To simplify the discussion presented herein, it will be assumed that the provision for the establishment of dimensions to provide for the container capability of the Universe, has already been done. Thus we will be dealing exclusively with the creation of the first something in the Universe.

Into our discussion at this point, we must introduce and consider certain qualities and attributes of God that are particularly pertinent to the initial creation approach. It will be found that for each different approach, a different set of these qualities and attributes will become especially applicable. For the initial creation approach, we shall have to consider the following conditions.

1. God created the Universe and everything in it.
2. God had to be in existence prior to the creation of the Universe.

3. God had an initial creation.

4. Because everything had to come after Him, God was the first something created.

5. Everything is derived from God. He is the fountainhead of all existence.

6. For anything to exist, God must exist. The maintenance of everything is through God.

7. God is all-powerful. All power of the Universe is through God.

8. He is a living God who meets the definition of being alive.

This list will be used to consider an approach involving a God derived from an initial creation. We will see how and if all this applies. We will use this approach to determine where it leads us. Finally we shall examine the consequences and implications of the resulting conclusions.

When we examine the possibility of an initial creation of the Universe, we find that there can be one and only one first step. Using the time-derived Equation of Existence (see the book of Existence for the full derivation) for this first step and using the appropriate terms, this equation becomes

$$4/3 \times = 1$$
$$\text{so that} \quad \times = 3/4 \quad \text{or} \quad 0.75000000$$

This is the first step and the first point of an initial creation, as it is expressed in mathematical terms. This is a very special point to which we will be concentrating much of our attention. This is the point to which we will be identifying the concept of the initial creation of God.

In an initial creation of the Universe, this point represents the very first something of all creation. This is the first something in the Universe. This verifies Item No. 4 from the previous list, which states that God was the first something created. Since this was the first creation, it also verifies Item No. 3 which states that God had an initial creation.

The mathematical value of this first point has been shown to be 0.75000000 which falls exactly in the geometric center of the Life (L) Range. When the included mathematics of an existence situation results in a numerical value that lies within the derived limits of the Life Range, the associated situation is said to meet the condition of life. Therefore, Item No. 8 is met wherein that which is being identified with God meets the definition of being alive.

After this first step of creation which establishes the first point (which is being identified to aspects of God), a second step is forthcoming which involves the establishment of three points wherein each represents separately the precise working centers respectively of the Energy (E), Life (L), and Matter (M) Ranges. Together these E-L-M Ranges make up all of the total existence in the Universe.

With the three points of the second step established, the development of the Universe continues with an ordered series of subsquent steps. Each step has its own set of included points. The relationships of these steps and their points are described in more detail in Chapter 23 entitled "Concept of the Repeating Cyclical Universe."

The importance of these ordered steps of existence is that they show that all existence goes through and is developed after the first step is established. Since Step 1 is identified with aspects of God, Item No. 2 is now verified since it is shown that God had to be in existence prior to the creation of the Universe. In addition, because this first step is essential and all following creation is based upon its being there, Item No. 1 is met by referencing everything that follows, God created the Universe and everything in it.

From these it follows that Items 5, 6, and 7 can now be met. Point one of Step one must be and continue to be in order to derive and maintain all that follows. Thus God is truly the fountainhead of all existence. Since all energy of the universe is developed through Step 1, all power of the Universe is through God.

Finally it should be remembered that Step 1 is not only the primary existence point of the Universe and the first point of time, it is the dynamic or initial creation point of God as well.

8

THE STEADY-STATE EXISTENCE CONCEPT OF GOD

"He is everything that has come into existence,
And what will come into being in eternity."
(Hindu, Kaivalya Upanishad 8:9-10)

When Theology is discussed, it is the opinion of many people that God always existed in the Universe. Indeed, they reject any concept that God had a creation. Instead, they feel that there always was a God and that He is supreme and apart from any possible creation in the Universe. No matter what may happen, He is separated from that happening. He controls the events of the Universe. He directs them. But no matter how much change is involved, He can keep Himself separate and apart from that which actually does the changing. God is timeless, and yet He is all time. This then begins the examination of the steady-state existence concept of God.

The concept of something that involves the steady-state is in direct contrast to that of an initial creation. An initial creation infers something that includes extreme change and is thus dynamic. Something that involves a condition of being steady-state implies a relatively changeless situation and is thus considered to be static. To say that something is static implies a stability to the subject entity.

In addition to dealing with God, we are also dealing with the Universe. Except for the condition of Nothing, any existence in the Universe is subject to continual and complete change. In this framework, we must place and consider that which we call God.

As we did in the previous chapter, into our discussion at this point we must introduce those certain qualities and attributes of God that are particularly pertinent to the steady-state concept approach. While certain similarities may exist with the previous initial creation concept, the steady-state approach requires that its special list or set of qualities be developed. Accordingly, this list of items is as follows.

1. God has always existed and always will exist.
2. God is responsible for the creation of the Universe and everything in it.
3. Any and all change in the Universe is produced by God.
4. God is unaffected by any change in the Universe.
5. Whether or not there is a Universe is not relevant to the existence of God.

This approach involving the steady-state existence of God, requires a set of very unusual characteristics. God must be independent of the Universe itself. Certainly He must be independent of any creation or associated existence in the Universe. This concept, which is stated in Item No. 5, is absolutely essential so that God can meet the basic premise stated in Item No. 1.

The steady-state existence of God involves some very unusual and serious considerations. For God to be independent of the Universe (Item No. 5) and also to remain unaffected by any change therein (Item No. 4), means that God can not be in any part of the Universe. Thus God's existence must be somewhere outside of the Universe. By definition, the Universe extends into an infinity of geometric dimensions or dimensional groups. Therefore God can not be in any of these. The only place or location not covered by these is the Zero Dimension, which includes the state of Nothing. Thus that which we are calling the existence of God, must reside in the Realm of Nothing.

The Realm of Nothing has a special constituent which is highly significant in relation to the development of the steady-state concept of God. This special constituent is Time. Thus the concept known as Time is going to be identified with that concept known as God.

To understand this very important situation, we must have an understanding of the concept of Nothing. This is covered in detail in the book of Existence. First and probably the most obvious, the mathematical value of anything contained within or associated with the Realm of Nothing is zero. Since that which is being called God has been identified in this approach as being located within this realm, the steady-state God must have a numerical value of zero. When this is compared to each of the Energy (E), Life (L), and Matter (M) Ranges, there is no corresponding value in the respective E-L-M Tabulations. (See the book of EXISTENCE for these Tabulations.) Since these Tabulations define existence in all the dimensions of the Universe, the conclusion is that God has no direct existence in the Universe. The definition of Life states that to be alive, the associated mathematical value of the subject entity must lie within the limits of the Life Range. Since the numerical value of God in this approach does not lie in this Life Range, the steady-state concept of God does not meet the definition of Life so that God can not be alive herein.

The noumenon of Time has a special existence which has been identified within the Realm of Nothing. When the Curve of Existence and the separate Curve of Pre-Existence are examined for their Existence versus Time values at zero time, it is found that each curve shows a different value. This means that at its zero condition, the existence of time can be either of two values. Thus time at its zero condition has an inherent instability. There is a built-in tendency to produce a disturbance in the zero realm. Once started, this disturbance will initiate that which is called change in n-dimensional existence (where "n" is greater than zero). Thus the time disturbances produced in the zero realm are responsible for the referencing of all the included operations of the Universe.

Thus we have the capability to produce any and all change in the Universe. Since this was one of the qualities identified with God (see Item No. 3), Time itself (the noumenon of Time) is identified with the concept of God in this approach. Since it is an inherent characteristic of the Realm of Nothing, that which we call Time has always existed and, from all probability, will always exist as an operational entity. This again identifies with a quality attributable with the steady-state concept of God (see Item No. 1).

All operations in the Universe are referenced by concepts of Time. Creation and everything else in the Universe can be related to time-referenced operations. Therefore Item No. 2 is met since operations are related to time, time is related to God in this approach, and God then is responsible for the creation of the Universe and everything in it.

Within this Steady-State approach to the relationship of God in the Universe, there can be further mathematical interpretation. This approach presents the concept that there always was a God and that He is separate from anything and everything else, including the Universe. As such a separate and continuing entity, God can be said to be in parallel with the collective arrangement of everything else. Thus in the

Steady-State approach, the mathematical consideration of God would be identified as part of a parallel function.

This parallel aspect is in direct contrast to the Initial Creation approach (of Chapter 7) where in the Creation of the Universe the phenomenon of God must be created prior to anything else. Thus in the sequence of the things created in the Universe in a predetermined specific order developed during the consideration of an Initial Creation, God came first (see Chapter 6). By His coming first in the entire sequence of the happenings occurring in an Initial Creation approach, the associated mathematical consideration of God would be identified as part of a series function.

9

THE THINKING PROCESS AND THE ADVANCED WISDOM OF GOD

"Not by speech, not by thought,
Not by sight can He be realized.
How can He be understood
Otherwise than by saying 'He is'?"
(Hindu, Katha Upanishad I:13)

So far, we have examined the major two approaches concerning the existence of God. Since each particular format necessitated a specific premise (initial creation or steady-state), it was required that an associated set of characteristics and aspects be considered for each one. Though there was some overlap, each set was essentially different from the other. When these sets are examined, it will be noted that there is an important omission. One of the most important attributes of God is not included. There is no provision in either of the previously presented concepts to allow for the necessary *wisdom* of God. Not only has this quality for wisdom been left out, there is actually no possibility whatsoever that this characteristic can be included in either previous approach to provide for this required capability of God.

Before proceeding further, let us examine what is meant

by the concept of Wisdom. To have wisdom implies that there must be thought. Thought is tied in to the thinking process. The thinking process involves multi-dimensional operations.* The memory portion is always located in a dimensional group that comes prior to the one containing that which is called a brain. For the human being, the brain is located in association with the physical presence in the first dimensional group while the conventional memory is located in the second dimensional group. Thus at least two separate dimensional groups must be involved to perform the general operations associated with the thinking process.

The initial creation and the steady-state concepts of God have no provisions for a thinking process. In the initial creation concept, the identification of God was made to the first time point or creation point in the Universe. At this first point, by definition, there is nothing before it so that there is no prior dimensional group to permit the location of the memory requirement. Thus there can be no complete thinking process for the God developed in the initial creation concept.

In the steady-state concept, the associated location of God was placed in the zero dimension. That which is called the brain can not exist in the zero dimension. Thus there can be no possibility of a thinking process for the God developed in the steady-state concept.

It should be noted that the initial creation and the steady-state concepts are the two major theories dealing with the existence of God. Therefore

DUE TO THE LACK OF AN INCLUDED THINK-ING PROCESS, BOTH THE INITIAL CREATION AND THE STEADY-STATE CONCEPTS OF GOD ARE CONSIDERED TO BE UNACCEPTABLE IN THEIR PRESENT FORM.

* See the book of LIFE

86

Without a thinking process to perform the necessary operations, it becomes most apparent that there is certainly no capability for any wisdom in these two approaches.

The need now arises to obtain a useful theological approach that can provide God with the capability for attaining wisdom. Surprisingly among most of the major theological concepts, this area has been lacking in development. Most of the religions assign great wisdom to their God who has somehow acquired this capability during an apparently long but undescribed period of existence. When each religion first mentions its God, He usually has all His attributes and capabilities at this point in time.

But one major religion does attempt to look into these fundamental questions and aspects. That religion is Hinduism. Similarly to the other great religions, the Hindu religious writings point out the extreme difficulty in trying to understand that which we call God. They state

> Not by speech, not by thought,
> Not by sight can He be realized.
> How can He be understood
> Otherwise than by saying "He is"?
> (Katha Upanishad I:13)

The supreme God of Hinduism is called Brahma. In the sacred writings, He is considered from many points of view including the steady-state existence.

> "Great Brahma is without an earlier and without a later."
> (Maitri Upanishad VI:17)

In addition, the possibility of an Initial Creation was also considered. The following quotation represents the last stanza of the Creation Hymn of the Rig Veda (see Chapter 2 herein for a more complete translation of this important Hindu Scripture).

"This creation, from whence did it come into existence?
Was it made by itself, or was it not.
He who sees all in highest heaven,
Surely He knows—or perhaps He knows it not."

(Rig Veda X:129)

This Hindu Creation Hymn is quite unusual in its content. The statement about Creation involving the question "Was it made by itself" is especially interesting since it suggests and implies the elimination of God from the Creation process. It additionally bears directly upon the contents of Chapter 23 presented herein which is entitled "Concept of the Repeating Cyclical Universe."

It is the last concept presented in the Creation Hymn which is considered to be the most thought provoking. Discussing God at Creation, it says ". . . perhaps He knows it not." This backs up the statement presented at the beginning of this chapter which questioned the thinking capability of God to operate during the previously considered two approaches. Since the Rig-Veda is estimated to be over 4,000 years old, it is interesting to note that the ancient Hindus also mentioned the possibility of a lack of knowledge on God's part in connection with the initial creation and the steady-state situations of the Primordial Universe.

With such extensive capabilities for insight on the part of the Hindus, it is especially useful to examine some of their views concerning the development of the wisdom of God. Indeed one Hindu sect has come up with an extraordinary interpretation which will be used herein to serve as the basis for the next approach that we will consider.

If there is to be a supreme Being, a God, then it is necessary that He have supreme wisdom. But to have supreme wisdom requires the most superior of Beings with the most sophisticated and the most advanced type of thinking process. In the hierarchy of the development of life after the creation of the Universe and the Earth, the first forms had very simple brains with very simple types of thinking processes. As time went on, the various forms of life became larger with increasingly complex structures. The included brains and the associated capabilities for thinking became more and more sophisticated. Along this sequence of events came man and his higher developed capabilities. But a God is greater than man. Therefore in the hierarchy of the development of life, God had to be created *after* the development of man. This makes the creation of God one of the latter creations in the Universe. Only then could a supreme Being be developed with the superior brain and thinking system capable of attaining the supreme wisdom.

But if God, the supreme Being, was created *after* man, how was the Universe created? Indeed from a theological point of view, who was responsible for the creation of the Universe?

This Hindu sect has an answer to this with an ordered pantheon of Gods. They believe that there are many many Gods, each having a responsibility for certain operations and activities. Creation and the full associated range of activities were carried on and performed by various Gods of the total group. Eventually, from this collective group, one God (Brahma) emerged supreme. It is this supreme God who has acquired and attained the necessary complete and supreme wisdom. In the words from the Upanishads,

"He is everything that has come into existence,
And what will come into being in eternity."
                                        (Kaivalya Upanishad 8:9-10)

Thus this Hindu concept is that it takes a long period of time for a God to acquire that unusual mental capability that we call wisdom. But by this concept, there is a most unique implication concerning creation. This implication is that

THE ACT OF CREATION
DOES NOT REQUIRE ANY WISDOM.

Again this supports the conclusions of the last two presented chapters. These initial creation and steady-state approaches implied that there was no thinking process possible or available to God in the associated creation of the Universe. This means that the creation of the Universe had to be handled and governed by other principles. Indeed such means are presented and discussed in Chapter 23 entitled "Concept of the Repeating Cyclical Universe." It states that prescribed steps, defined by precise mathematical terminology developed by specific equations, are in effect during an Initial Creation and all associated phases that come to follow. By this process, no outside influence of any kind is possible. These steps are predetermined and therefore required in an exact order to happen after each completed sequence of the previous step. Indeed upon the destruction or Termination of the Universe, the entire process and sequence of steps would be subject to repetition. Thus the development of the Universe is automatically constrained to occur by *definition*, not by outside influence.

If that which we call wisdom does not enter into the beginning of a process, it does have effects upon the end operations. The described Hindu concepts consider that God attains wisdom well after the Universe has been established. The human being apparently operates in much the same way. At the moment of birth, a human being has a relatively undeveloped thinking process. Certainly there is no capacity for any wisdom at this time. As time passes, the included thinking capability begins and continues to develop through formal learning and actual experiences. If all this continues in a positive capacity, the thinking ability is enhanced. If there is sufficiency of this mental development, then the beginnings of wisdom can be said to occur and continue. When (and if) this occurs will vary from person to person. In almost all cases, this associated occurrence will take place when the human being has developed into adulthood.

Thus wisdom for the human being will come well after his time of creation. This correlates with the concept of God attaining His wisdom well after the Universe has been established. This concept is of special significance because it can be related to the fact that the number of the steps counted in the predetermined development of the Universe, have reached very high numerical values when that which is called wisdom occurs.

Each step includes a set of time points whose total number (p) increases as the step number (s) increases, in accordance with the relationship

$$p = 3 \, (2)^{s-2}$$

See Chapter 23 entitled "Concept of the Repeating Cyclical Universe" for more discussion. Thus as the step number of development becomes very high, the associated number of time points available becomes huge. Since these time points have been identified with concepts of Free Will, they also become important and necessary aspects of the thinking process. Thus the capability for thinking is greatly improved as greater numbers of these time points are made available. When, for each step set, the number of included time points reaches a high enough number, then the capability for wisdom is reached.

This can be compared to an electronic computer that is intended to perform very complex operations. The capability to do this effectively must be designed into the main operational portion, which in a conventional logic computer is known as the Central Processing Unit (CPU). Here facilities must be provided to allow for the complex processings. Complexity can be equated to how extensive the processings must be. Therefore, more places in the CPU must be provided to handle the extensive operations. These places are known as "Registers." These registers in the computer can be compared to the time points in the human thinking process. The more that are available, the greater the depth and detail to which a problem can be analyzed. (Of course, all the necessary other elements and portions must also be present in sufficient quantity to allow for the completion of the processing.)

Thus wisdom can only occur when the thinking process has reached a high enough operational level. It can only come toward the latter portions of the development of the entity, whether that be a man, a Universe, or a God.

10

ADVANCED CONCEPT OF AN OMNIPOTENT GOD

"But we speak the wisdom of God in a mystery, even the hidden wisdom, which God ordained before the world unto our glory:"
(The Bible, N.T., 1 Corinthians 2:7)

Each of the previous discussions concerning the existence of God has resulted in the pointing up of the serious omissions. In both the initial creation and the steady-state approaches, the presented God not only lacked wisdom but in addition, it was shown that there was no possibility of any kind for a thinking process. For the initial creation approach, God met the definition of life but under no circumstances could the God of the steady-state approach be considered alive. When the capability for supreme wisdom was developed for God, it was found that He could not have been responsible for the creation of the Universe. Thus in each previous approach, the developed God was far from omnipotent with important capabilities distinctly and definitely missing.

Now we shall concentrate upon an approach using the

premise of an omnipotent God. For the development of this approach, we shall see what attendant concepts and conditions are required to allow for meeting the premise. Especially, we shall see what time concepts are involved.

First let us describe what is meant by an omnipotent God. Specifically, an omnipotent God will possess those characteristics and capabilities that are considered to be most important in terms of this and the previous approaches as well. These include just a relatively small number of basic capabilities and powers. More cannot be included because a startling problem comes up. The powers that can actually be ascribed to God are limited. God is not actually omnipotent. Rather it will be shown that there are very few powers that can be assigned to a so-called omnipotent God.

When the powers of God are examined, it will be seen that these can not be unlimited. For example, could God create something so big that He could not control it? Here the limitation is quite evident. Could there be power over something that does not exist? If power is to be applied or exerted, the subject upon which this power is to be directed, must be said to exist. Thus if something does not exist, there can be no end influence or effect of directed power. A something must exist to be affected by power.

But this requirement poses a further problem. In the book of EXISTENCE, there are mathematical derivations which show that the Universe does not exist for all practical purposes. This could eliminate any possibility of control by a deity. Fortunately, existence can be established on a theoretical basis. Thus for all theoretical purposes, the Universe can be said to exist on a theoretical basis. Within this framework, existence can also be established for Energy (E), Life (L), and Matter (M) on a time-derived basis. Thus it can be said that there is a Universe and that this Universe can be described in terms of Energy, Life, and Matter which have existences within the derived E-L-M Tabulated Ranges (see the book of EXISTENCE).

With the formal establishment of the Universe, there results something upon which power can be exerted. But as presented herein (see Chapter 23 entitled "Concept of the Repeating Cyclical Universe"), the developmental steps of the Universe are predetermined and fixed in prescribed patterns.

NO OUTSIDE INFLUENCE
CAN AFFECT THESE STEPS.

Therefore, no outside power from a Deity or anything else can have any effect upon the operations of these steps.

During the beginning phases of an Initial Creation of the Universe, all associated operations are fixed to happen in prescribed patterns of steps. Nothing can change the order of these steps. Therefore, no Deity can alter or influence these steps in any way. Once the creation has started, God can have no powers or capabilities over the associated operations. Again the powers of God are limited.

As the Universe (or any creation) continues in its development, it increases in geometrical structure and operational complexity. While the steps in the development occur in fixed prescribed patterns, there are a number of points between the steps that allow for a certain degree of freedom. Each set or group of points between adjacent steps must have their associated operations completed before the next step is invoked. However, there is relative freedom to the order in which the points are completed. Thus the concept of Predestination can be identified with the steps while the concept of Free Will can be identified with the points.

In the beginning of the development of any creation, Predestination is the dominant mode of operation because of the fixed ordering of the steps and because of the relatively few associated points. As the development continues, the associated number of points increases exponentially until the points become the basis as the dominant mode of operation. When this occurs, Free Will is said to be in effect.

In a sequence of operations which follows the aspects and conditions associated with the Equation of Existence (see the book of Existence), the crossover point which separates the dominant realms of Predestination from Free Will, is located one-eighth (1/8) of the way (measured from the starting end) of the entire sequence range. The mathematical relationship involving the associated function was first noted in the book of LIFE, in the chapter entitled "The Derivation of Sex." This same one-eighth relationship has now been identified with

1. Matter—separation point between Helium and Lithium in the Periodic Table of the Chemical Elements.

2. Life—separation point in Life entities noted in the Life Tabulation after which reproduction functions are divided into two groups associated with Male and Female.

3. Energy—separation point in the Energy Tabulation which marks the initiation of Light.

4. Life development—separation point between childhood and adulthood.

5. Thinking—separation point in the life span of thinking creatures after which organized thinking is said to take place.

6. Brain development—separation point in the Life Tabulation after which a brain is said to be in operation.

7. Operations Control—separation point between Pre-

destination (associated with initial development) and Free Will (associated with continued further development).

For our immediate discussion, the aspects of thinking and Free Will shall be emphasized in connection with this one-eighth (1/8) relationship. The demarcation location of this 1/8 relationship is also known as the "Sex Point" in honor of the derivation in which it was discovered. As the associated operations continue further, past this point the capabilities for thinking and Free Will come into being.

Thinking implies a process. Free Will implies a certain freedom in the exercising of the thinking process. The continued development of thinking can lead to additional utilization and improvement. As this improvement continues, a point is reached where it can be said that wisdom has occurred. Wisdom can be defined as the capability to provide for reasonably complete organized use of thinking to relate to and deal with numerous and varied kinds of problems. For wisdom to occur, organized thinking must be performed in grouped operations which are developed and arranged in patterns. Then pattern recognition techniques are utilized to produce the highly organized and formal results that are associated with that which we call "wisdom."

In the sequence of operations which follows the aspects and conditions associated with the Equation of Existence, the crossover point which separates the realms of ordinary thinking from wisdom is located one-half (1/2) of the way along the entire sequence range. From multi-dimensional considerations, this half-way point can be identified with several relationships.

1. It separates the conventional Euclidean 3-dimensional space from other dimensional groups.
2. It provides for the development of the mathemati-

97

cal function $f(\pi/4)$ to allow for circular geometric shapes.

3. It separates the realm of ordinary Free Will thinking operations from the realm of organized Free Will thinking.

4. It provides for the thinking capability called wisdom.

5. In multi-dimensional notation, it marks the point where light energy appears in the primary dimensional group.

For our immediate discussion, the aspect of wisdom will be emphasized in connection with this one-half (1/2) relationship noted with respect to the E-L-M Tabulations. The demarcation location of this 1/2 relationship will also be known as the "Wisdom Point" in connection with the concept in which it was developed. As the associated activities continue further past this wisdom point in the overall sequence of operations, the capabilities for wisdom come into being.

As operations continue in the tabulated sequences beyond the wisdom point, the next point of consequence to be considered herein is located 7/8 of the way (measured from the starting end) along the entire sequence range. This is known as the "Phase Out Point" because it marks the end of the major operational range. In the realm beyond this point, all activities and that which is called existence will move into the termination phase. This 7/8 relationship can be identified with:

1. The termination of an existence sequence.

2. The range of 1/8 to 7/8 which represents the extent of the existence of the primary group. When the value of 1/8 is subtracted from 7/8, the result is 3/4 which represents the proportion of the distribution of exis-

tence which is considered to be present in the primary dimensional group.

3. The range of 1/2 to 7/8 which represents the extent of the conventional Euclidean 3-dimensional range in the multi-dimensional interpretation of the E-L-M Tabulations.

4. For Matter—the end of the stable elements.

5. For Energy—the demarcation point before the beginning of the radio-active type energies.

6. For multi-dimensional notation—the point noting that the First, Second, and Third Dimensional Groups have all associated operational steps and points completed and filled.

The mechanism form for the termination aspect of the 7/8 point is developed in Item 6 above. On the E-L-M Tabulations,* the 7/8 point falls between Ref. Nos. 448 and 449. Here the Sig-Group moves into the 3-4-5 dimensions for the first time in the sequence. This signifies that the main positions in the most important dimensions are filled. All remaining operations will be performed in the higher order dimensions. These remaining operations will be done in the last 1/8 of the tabulation sequence.

With the 3-4-5 dimensional positions completed, the process associated with final aging sets in. Thus the final 1/8 phase involves the termination of the activities in the primary dimensional group.

From the previous discussions herein, three major points (the Tri-Point Concept) have been identified to be associated with a sequence of operations. These include the points at the 1/8, 1/2, and 7/8 locations. In addition to the E-L-M Tabulations, these points can be used with any complete mathematical series or full tabulated sequence. They repre-

* See the book of EXISTENCE

sent the full major range of activities that can mathematically occur in any primary dimensional group under consideration. They also represent a summary of the applicable values of a complete set of time-derived functions obtained and developed within the book of Time.

Now we shall use all this for the summary objective of developing an omnipotent God.

In the proposed exploring of any considered activity or subject, it is necessary to first define and establish the characteristics and capabilities associated with that included subject. Most of the time, this is a reasonably straightforward activity. But in this case, God as a distinct subject represents something of the very highest order of complexity and nebulosity. And it is required to provide a definition representation of an omnipotent God.

We shall start with a listing of the powers that might be anticipated. As the word "omnipotent" implies, God shall be considered as being all-powerful. But as the three previous chapter discussions have shown, there will be limitations in this area.

Next we shall list some of the more important characteristics of God. These shall provide the initial conditions to reference this development. These shall include:

1. Existence—God must be said to exist.

2. Continuity—The being of God must continue regardless of the existence of the Universe.

3. Spiritual Presence—Within the existence of the Universe, there must be a manifestation means for a spiritual presence.

4. Life—Within the existence framework of the Universe, the included Deity must be a living God.

5. Immortality—The life qualities of the Deity shall be perpetual, undying, everlasting, and shall not be sub-

ject to any deteriorating effects associated with mortal existence.

6. Wisdom—There shall be the quality to exercise good judgment through organized thinking.

7. Purpose—There should be direction, meaning, and reasons associated with the efforts and being of the Deity.

Now let us examine each of these items in further detail.

When it is said that God must exist, the concepts of Existence Theory (see book of Existence) must be used for comparison and interpretation. For something to exist, it must do so within the framework of an existent environment. When it is established that there is a Universe, we have a suitable framework. Indeed the initial creation point of the Universe provides an exact geometric reference location that has the relationship capability for a significant identification with that which we call God (see chapter 7 entitled "Initial Creation and the Creation of God" herein). This relationship is suitable when there is a Universe. But what happens under the conditions of no Universe such as would be prevalent prior to the Creation and after the Termination of that which is known as the Universe? Can we allow for an existence of God under such circumstances? The direct answer to this question is "No," but there is an indirect approach which must be explored.

If we go back to the very basics of Physics, it will be found that there is non-existence prior to the establishment of existence. Non-existence can also be identified with the zero state or zero existence which is called out when dealing with the formal concepts of Nothing. Here any attempts to consider or provide for order, will be referenced by definition and not by design. In the basic concepts related to the non-existent state of Nothing, there is no geometry possible by definition. Thus there can be no points or locations for any attempted identification with God. However, the entire non-existent region considered as a total aspect could be presented as a general location.

There is an unusual characteristic of the non-existent region which bears directly upon our problem and can provide for the continuity of the Deity. The non-existent region represents the repository for the noumenon of time. Within this region can be found the instability previously determined by the mathematical definition of Nothing. When the domains of existence and non-existence are studied and compared, it will be found that there is a common boundary zone which appears at the common point of zero. At this point, each of the two domains has a different mathematical value. Thus two different states of zero can be in operation. This condition represents a distinct discontinuity in the function of zero or f(O). The two different states of zero will separately form across the discontinuity. The included situation is unstable so that either value can variously be in effect.

This instability in the non-existent Realm of Zero represents the noumenon of Time. The instability causes a continual switching back and forth between two different mathematical states. These switching operations represent repeating 2-state changes which result in disturbances in the non-existent realm. The disturbances manifested in the realm of non-existence will also result in disturbances in any other realms depending upon the availability of their existence. Thus these f(O) disturbances in the domain of non-existence will directly cause carry-over effects in other available realms. These carry-over effects produce associated disturbances which then can set up the aspects and conditions necessary for initiating changes. Thus while the f(O) disturbances in the non-existent domain represent the noumenon of Time, the correspondingly produced changes in the existence domain represent the phenomenon of Time.

This conjugate pair (noumenon-phenomenon) concept of Time provides the means to allow for the continuity of God in the absence of an existent Universe. In a like manner to Time, God has a conjugate continuity in the realms of existence and non-existence. This conjugate continuity provides the extension capabilities necessary to bridge and extend into any possibility and combination of various types of existences.

That this is so can be seen by examining the attendant conditions surrounding and associated with an initial creation. By definition, an initial creation involves an extension and a change from a non-existence into a something that can be identified with an existence. In this context of an initial creation, non-existence and existence represent a conjugate pair. Thus an existence represents an extension originating out of a non-existence. Since an existence is a resulting effect or manifestation, it can be described as a phenomenon. The associated origin located in the realm of non-existence represents the noumenon. Thus the noumenon of Time is located in the realm of non-existence. In corresponding manner, the noumenon of God must be identified with the same realm.

The importance of the conjugate relationship, is that God must be considered in accordance with this concept. The origin of God is in the realm of non-existence. All operations and activities must have their original initiation in this realm. Whether or not there is a Universe or any other existence, is inconsequential. The noumenon of God is maintained regardless of any outside conditions. Thus the continuity of the being of God is established.

The Spiritual Presence represents the means for the manifestation of God. When it is said that God exists, that existence is identified with just one point in the Universe. This is the Initial Creation point, the first point in the Universe. It represents the fountainhead of all existence. From this one point, everything else occurs. This point is the very first step in the formal ordering of the Universe.

From this one vantage point in the formal ordering of the Universe, it is necessary for God to have the capability of manifesting Himself throughout the entire system of the Universe. It has been presented (see Chapter 11 entitled "Concept of the Soul") that that which is the guiding reference of life, has its presence in the previous dimensional group. This reference presence is known as the Soul and has some existence distribution association separately with each and every life form. Thus each life has an extension of its existence in a previous dimensional group. This leads to yet another conjugate pair—life and its soul. Since the soul is the reference and the life is its manifestation, the soul is the noumenon and life is the phenomenon.

All of life has a common origin which is traceable back to the initial creation point which is geometrically identified with God. This indeed makes ". . . God, the firstborn of every creature" (Colossians 1:15). As more and more life forms are created and developed, the extension from the initial creation point becomes greater and greater. From this aspect, the resulting manifestation capability of God becomes greater and greater. From this point of view

"He is everything that has come into existence,
And what will come into being in eternity."
(Kaivalya Upanishad 8:9-10)

It is the stated belief of some, that each person is the "I AM" of God. In this interpretation, God is manifesting Himself separately through each and every person. Therefore, the efforts of God are spread and operated through each and every form of life to promote and effect His Will. This collective operation through the souls or references of life provides the mechanism for the Spiritual Presence, thereby allowing for the manifestation of God. Since each soul represents the noumenon of its associated life, the mechanism of the Spiritual Presence operates through the totality of the collective noumena of all life.

The concept of life has been invoked in connection with the interpretation of God. To operate within the realm of existence, God would have to be some form of life. On the more technical basis, that which has been defined as God would have to meet the mathematical definition of life. The initial creation point is defined as the first something to be created in the Universe and is the first point of existence. The aspect of God associated with existence in the Universe, has already been identified with this point (see chapter 7 entitled "Initial Creation and the Creation of God"). Indeed, the mathematical valuation of this point (0.75000000) is exactly at the geometric center of the developed Life Range of the L-Tabulation. Thus this time-derived interpretation of God specifically meets the mathematical definition of life.

Immortality is a further requirement that must be met. The previous requirement for continuity necessitates that the life aspect of God be perpetual. This means that within the realm of existence, there must be a continuum of the life qualities of God without any of the deteriorating effects usually associated with mortal existence. Since life is only associated with that which is called existence, the immortality is only required to be in effect for as long as the Universe continues to exist.

The geometrical location of God in the Existence Continuum of the Universe is at the Initial Creation Point. This first point in the Universe is not affected by the deteriorating operations to which the later points are subjected. Indeed, all later points buffer the Initial Creation Point from all the usual outside effects. When change occurs, it does so usually and mostly at the outside steps and points on the periphery of the Existence Continuum. Therefore, there will be an absolute minimum of effects to this Initial Creation Point caused by outside change. Thus the intrinsic aspect of life will be preserved and the concept of immortality can be said to be in effect.

The requirement for God to have wisdom presents what may be the most difficult problem of all. For wisdom is a special formal situation that is attained through advanced organized thinking. Thus wisdom requires that the capability of a thinking process be available as a basic minimum. But thinking involves a multi-dimensional operation for its methodology and completion. The included geometry associated with the primary or conjugate concept of God, just does not allow for the operations of a basic thinking process. The primordial God has no capability for thinking whatsoever. Thus there is no possibility for wisdom at this level.

Since thinking involves a multi-dimensional geometry, then such a geometrical environment must exist before the operation of thinking can be performed. Accordingly this associates thinking with existence and with the formal aspects of a Universe. It was mentioned earlier that thinking is said to start at the 1/8 point while wisdom as a capability is said to start at the 1/2 point, as related to the developed Life Range as presented in the mathematical L-Tabulations.* Again this points up the geometrical requirement for the Existence Continuum of the Universe, which is needed to support particular operations. For the wisdom requirement of God to occur, it could only begin at the half-way point in the development of the Universe. Thus the direct capability for wisdom would be lacking during the first half of the development of the Universe.

There is a secondary means through which wisdom could

* See the book of EXISTENCE

be developed and exercised. This secondary access could be considered as being part of the methodology associated with aspects of the Spiritual Presence. Since the origin of all life is traceable to the initial creation point (which has been identified with God), the thinking potential of all life could be considered as being accessible and usable by God. Therefore, the wisdom of God can be said to be the sum total of the available collective wisdom of all life with advanced thinking systems that, in turn, meet the definition of wisdom. The question of purpose has special significance in any study relating to the concepts associated with Theology. Of all the concepts considered herein, purpose represents a subject which is neither a characteristic nor a capability. Rather it poses a problem concerning whether there is any reason that might be ascribed to having a Deity. Even if there is purpose, is it possible to ascertain what it is?

We have just determined that wisdom is not present in the primordial aspect of God. Therefore, there can be no beginning purpose. The order in the Universe is by definition and not by design. Thus there is no thinking or decision-making involved in the ordered relationships or the predestined steps of the Universe. However, after the half-way point of development, the capability for wisdom becomes available. Since the beginning has already been excluded, then the direction that the development of the Universe is taking must have some bearing. Thus if there is truly some Divine purpose, then

THERE MUST BE DIVINE DESTINATION
RATHER THAN DIVINE ORIGIN.

Therefore, there must be some Divine end purpose in Theology for the Universe. Again the concept of the conjugate pair is invoked for this interpretation. The Universe represents the manifestation of the totality of the phenomena devel-

107

oped by God in accordance with Theology. If the Universe is the phenomenon, then the purpose must involve the destination of the associated noumenon. Therefore, the purpose is the Universe, the manifestation of the thing in itself.

If the purpose is the Universe, then the specific powers of God are intended for that purpose. The question is—What powers does God specifically have? In examining such powers, it is important to realize that these can not be infinite. There must be definite limitations on everything, even the powers associated with a Deity. All things are limited by the attendant conditions associated with their being and presence. For example, could something be created that was so big that it could not be controlled? In this statement, limitations are seen that affect creation, size, and control. Beyond certain limits, there must be an incompatibility among these three stated parameters.

In examining power, this power can only be exercised over that which is said to exist. If there was no Universe, then no power could be exerted over it. When a Universe is created, power can then be applied but only in limited amounts depending upon the overall extent of what is actually considered to exist. Thus the maximum amount of power that can be applied is proportional to the actual existence that is available. Any power that is applied must itself be said to exist. Therefore this power must come from the energy potential already in existence. Energy (E), like Life (L) and Matter (M), follows an order of development in accordance with the presentations listed in the E-L-M Tabulations (see the book of EXISTENCE). At specific steps in the development of the Universe, only certain limited amounts of Energy are available. Thus the amount of power for use by a Deity is definitely limited.

As the Universe develops, it can only do so in specific prescribed steps. The order of these steps is by definition and not by any outside design or influence. Thus a Deity does not

108

have any power to affect this prescribed order. This is further shown in various religious scriptures where the described happenings, once set into effect, can never be altered. If God does not have full control over the operations of the Universe, and His powers are limited, then what powers are actually ascribed to God? The one remaining category is the power of sudden, drastic, or catastrophic change. Mathematically, this is represented by the step function which is a sudden switching of levels. It is a digital rather than an analog change. It results in something that is distinctly different from that which went before.

Stated in general terms, the actual and only powers of God are CREATION and TERMINATION. God can initiate and He can end.

"... the Lord gave, and the Lord hath taken away;"
(The Bible, O.T., Job 1:21)

Consider what God has actually done in accordance to the various religious scriptures. He has created the heavens and the earth. He has created man and woman. He has initiated the Flood of 40 days and 40 nights associated with the time of Noah. He destroyed Sodom and Gomorrah. He caused the seven plagues to befall the Egyptians. He parted the Red Sea for the Israelites.

All of these examples illustrate sudden activities involving drastic changes. In fact, when God is called upon or invoked, it usually is for some drastic reason that requires a sudden or a complete change of some included subject situation. Thus the main, and actually the only power of God, involves change.

But change is synonymous with the concept of Time. So we find that the only power of God is identified with the concept of Time.

So far, we have not been emphasizing the importance of

109

Time and Time Theory. Yet the concepts of Time have appeared again and again. Let us review these concepts and list them now.

1. In the realm of existence, the location of God has been identified with the initial creation point of the Universe, which is also the first time point in the Universe.

2. In the realm of non-existence, the origin and more importantly, the noumenon of God has been placed. From Time Theory, the noumenon of Time is also located in the realm of non-existence. Since the realm of non-existence has no dimension, this realm is a region of zero size and therefore it is just represented by a point of zero dimension. Since the noumenon of God and the noumenon of Time are both located in this point of zero dimension, they are both synonymous with each other. Therefore the noumenon of God is identified with the noumenon of Time.

3. Due to the identification with the initial creation point of the Universe and the location in the realm of non-existence, the conjugate or dual relationship of God is the same as the conjugate or dual relationship of Time. The noumenon-phenomenon of God is the same as the noumenon-phenomenon of Time.

4. As a living entity in the Universe, the existence and operations of God follow the prescribed pattern of time points.

5. The quality of immortality and the concept of Time are both eternal.

6. Regardless of the existence of a Universe, the concepts of God and of Time both have continuity. Nothing else meets this particular situation.

7. The Spiritual Presence is manifested through Time operations.

8. The conjugate pair for all life is the soul/living presence relationship. The soul is the reference and the noumenon of life. Since God has been identified as a form of life (in existence), He must have a soul. Therefore,

THE SOUL OF GOD IS IDENTIFIED WITH
THE NOUMENON OF TIME.

The conclusion of this interpretation of an omnipotent God is most definite. God and Time are synonymous. That which has been called God has the exact qualities and aspects as that which is called Time. All Time Theory can be compared very favorably with corresponding aspects of Theology. The conclusion is inescapable. If it is said that there is a God, then

GOD AND TIME ARE ONE AND THE SAME.

Part III

THE SOUL

11

CONCEPT OF THE SOUL

". . . a man be born of water and of the Spirit,"
(The Bible, N.T., John 3:5)

One of the subject areas that has been extremely difficult to discuss is the concept of the human Soul. Due to a lack of the necessary intellectual tools, this subject has remained most obscure. It has been labelled as abstract in nature and its elusiveness has defied definition and detailed examination. Now with the new concepts of Time Theory and Existence Theory, the means are available to explore this unusual area to provide useful information and interpretation.

Since this subject of the human Soul is so very complex, it will be necessary to go into a higher degree of organization than has been used in dealing with the simpler topics. For this purpose, it is desirable to begin by introducing a special word to help with the analysis. This word is "Noumenon." It will be used to aid in pinpointing exactly what it is that we mean when we use the concept of the Soul.

To explain the word "Noumenon," we shall make use of its conjugate word which is "Phenomenon." In this conjugate pair usage, the noumenon deals with the subject while the phenomenon refers to what the subject does. Everyone at some time or other has looked up into the night skies to observe the magnificence of the stars. Yet no one has ever seen a star because their actual presence is always obscured by the intense light that they emit. All we can see is the light emanation which represents the phenomenon of the star. Thus we see what the star does, but not what it is. The subject of the star (the noumenon or the thing in itself) is obscured and hidden by the phenomenon or what it does.

In essence, this is the problem that exists with the defining of the Soul. When we look at a human being, we see the physical manifestation or presence. But the Soul lies obscured and hidden. That which gives the real meaning to each life is considered to be the Soul. Thus the physical body represents the phenomenon of human life since it presents what the life does or how life appears. The Soul can be considered as the noumenon since it represents what life really is.

The great German philosopher Immanuel Kant (1724-1804) made use of the word noumenon in his writings. He went very deeply into a number of very difficult subjects to the point where he felt that some of these were inaccessible and beyond being experienced. He believed that these subjects could only be developed in the mind through a purely intellectual process involving nonsensuous intuition. Two of these subjects included the existence of God and the Soul, which he considered to be inherent in human life with the postulated characteristics of being self determining and immortal.

In order to develop useful understanding concerning the human Soul, a unique place to start is with an approach offered by Theology. Here life is usually defined as consist-

116

ing of two parts. These include the physical presence and something else which is described as being something apart from the physical. This something else is variously named the soul, spirit, or life force depending upon the particular religion that may be under consideration. Since that which is considered to be part of the real or physical is inferred to exist in conventional Euclidean 3-dimensional space, that which is apart from the physical implies existence somewhere else. That somewhere else implies existence in some other dimensional group or set of groups. This concept is taken up in much more detail in the book of EXISTENCE. Here concepts of Existence Theory and multi-dimensional geometry are presented and developed.

Existence Theory states that that which we call existence, has a distribution among a number of adjacent dimensional groups. If conventional Euclidean 3-dimensional space is defined as the first dimensional group, the Equation of Existence (see the book of EXISTENCE) will show that human life has relatively significant proportions of its existence distributed in the second and third dimensional groups. When we attempt a definition of the Soul, the associated existences in these second and third dimensional groups become likely candidates. According to concepts of personality presented in the book of LIFE, the imprint of the previous personality established at the moment of conception lies in the third group. The actual storage location associated with the human thinking process lies in the second group. It is the personality factor that has the greatest effect on dominating the life characteristics. Since it is the imprint effect that allows for the continuance of previous personalities, the location of the Soul is considered to be divided between these second and third dimensional groups.

So far, we have covered only the concepts related to Existence Theory. Now we shall bring in aspects of Time Theory. It is revealed in the book of LIFE that there are two memories operating at the moment of birth. One of these is the imprint of the composite effects of the previous personalities (Reincarnation Effect) which is established in the third dimensional group at the moment of conception. After its establishment, this memory represents a closed system which is not susceptible to change from the usual outside sources. The second memory is the conventional one of which most people are aware. This memory represents an open system that is susceptible and can be influenced by outside sources. This second memory is located in the second dimensional group.

As the human being continues its development from the moment of birth, the conventional or open memory acquires more and more data for storage. This conventional memory increases in its importance of being able to influence its associated life as it develops. Contrary to this, the imprinted memory located in the third dimensional group, after providing behavioral guides which are picked up as experience items by the conventional memory, continues to decrease in importance and actually fades away as time goes on. This fading away becomes significant to the human being at about the age of six years. The conventional memory is considered to be definitely dominant after approximately 12 years of age. Thus the location of the dominant function guiding its associated human life actually changes place during the included lifetime. Therefore, THE SOUL WILL BE LOCATED IN THE THIRD DIMENSIONAL GROUP UP UNTIL THE AGE OF SIX AND THEN WILL CHANGE SO THAT IT WILL BE LOCATED IN THE SECOND DIMENSIONAL GROUP AFTER THE AGE OF TWELVE.

The distribution of existence specifies mathematically what proportion of the total existence will be in each respective dimensional group. The physical presence in the first dimensional group (or conventional Euclidean 3-dimensional space) accounts for the major part of existence for any living form of life. While that which is called life continues, the first dimensional group will be considered operable. In this condition, all the extensions of existence in the various dimensional groups will be interacting with each other in what can be described as a CLOSED system. This means that operations of all the dimensional groups are so tied in with each other that there is almost no susceptibility to any interference from outside change effects. This is somewhat like the bonds of a good marriage. As long as this situation continues, there is little likelihood that any outside person could come in to cause unwanted change. Thus the good marriage could be called a closed system between the two people involved.

However, if one of the two people in this good marriage were to break away or die, the marriage would no longer be a closed system. Rather, one or both parties wuld be beyond the influence of the other so that they could be susceptible to outside effects. This would mean that the previously closed system was now OPEN. This situation could be applied to further describe a Life system.

Any system of life involves a distribution of the associated existence into a number of the multi-dimensional geometric groups included in the Universe. These geometries are needed to provide the containers so that which is said to exist, will have the place *where* it can exist. To make a pot of coffee, we first need the pot. Next we need a set of cups in which to place the completed coffee. Then we need additional places, such as people or sinks, so that we can finally dispense the coffee. The pot, the cups, the people (with their stomachs), the sinks—all these represent containers or geometries which can hold the particular existence called coffee. The completed coffee is distributed into a number of containers. Thus it can be said that through the dispensing of the finished coffee into a number of separate containers, there is a distribution of the existence of that which we called coffee.

For a system involving a life, its included existence is distributed into a number of containers. These containers are represented by the various separate geometries which we have called the multi-dimensional groups. Of these, the most obvious is the conventional Euclidean 3-dimensional space which we have called the first dimensional group. There are many other dimensional groups in which some portion of the overall existence is distributed. Right now, we will only consider the second and third groups.

The various dimensional groups have important characteristics and relationships which must be examined. When the distribution of existence is complete (i.e.—all major dimensional groups operational), interactions of various kinds will be taking place between the different multi-dimensional groups that make up the subject life system that is under study. For example, the memory or storage section of the human thinking process is located in the second dimensional group and works in conjunction with the physical brain located in the first dimensional group. This requires that there be definite interchange and interaction between the first and the second dimensional groups.

In addition to the interrelationships, each dimensional group has independent characteristics. Each represents a separate existence in itself. Although each is part of an overall distribution of existence, each is actually an individual entity. This situation is somewhat analogous to a freight train. The whole train represents the total existence. The individual cars make up the distribution of the train. Each of the individual cars of the train is a separate item in itself and thus can be considered to have its own existence. If the locomotive was disconnected from the rest of the train, the freight cars might not have an immediate means of propulsion, but they would still independently retain their own identities. Thus if portions of the freight train were missing, any separate remaining cars would still retain their own existence.

The concept of the distribution of existence of a life is

similar to the distribution of cars in a freight train. If the physical presence or body (which can be compared to the locomotive of a train) should die and thus cease to exist, the existences in the other dimensional groups would still retain their individual identity, at least for certain periods of time. In particular, the second and third dimensional groups are of special interest since they are (one or the other depending upon the age of the life under consideration) the repository of the Soul. If the subject life should die, the immediate major effect would be to terminate the physical presence in the first dimensional group. However, the other dimensional groups would continue to retain their respective existences. THUS THAT PORTION OF EXISTENCE THAT WE CALL THE SOUL WOULD CONTINUE TO EXIST EVEN AFTER THE TERMINATION OF THE PHYSI-CAL PRESENCE.

As long as the full distribution of existence was in effect, the associated life represented a CLOSED system wherein it was reasonably unsusceptible to outside influences. How-ever, upon termination of the physical presence (that which is called death), there will be a major portion missing from the overall existence. The remaining portions of the original existence will now be part of an OPEN system. That which was previously called the Soul will no longer be constrained but will now be relatively free to enter into new interactions. In this new uninhibited condition, it will be known by the new name of the SPIRIT. Thus

A SPIRIT IS DEFINED HEREIN
AS A DISEMBODIED SOUL.

When the subject life was fully operational, the Soul pro-vided the reference functions. When the subject life resulted in the termination of its physical presence, the regular re-straints were removed from the operations of the Soul.

121

Therefore, new capabilities and operational characteristics are extended to that which was called the Soul. With these new extra and open composite capabilities, there is a shift in this subject entity and it now becomes referred to as a "Spirit."

Once the included life is said to die, there is a termination of that portion of the total associated existence that was formerly in the first dimensional group. Even though this portion ceases in its existence, there will still be a continuation of the existences in the other dimensional groups. That which was the Soul in the full or closed life system, now becomes the Spirit in the open or remaining system. This Spirit will continue as long as there is significant existence within its particular dimensional group. Thus there will be a continuance of the Soul in the new form as a Spirit.

Now the question must be asked—How long does the Spirit continue to exist? There are actually two answers to this question which are conditional depending upon which path and accompanying circumstances are considered. The first, considers the Spirit with no change. The second possible answer, considers the Spirit involved in a composite imprint upon a new life at the moment of conception, wherein the Spirit reverts to becoming part of the Soul of the new life. In both of these cases, that which is known as the Spirit will continue to exist almost indefinitely.

In the first case, the aspect of the spirit is formed into the existence of the dimensional group in which it was developed. As such, it remains in this form in an almost unchanged condition. It should be noted that the second and third dimensional groups do not have change operations similar to that of the first dimensional group. The usual capabilities for massive change and decay are just not present. So as long as there is no change in the relative significance of the formation geometry with respect to the actual distribution of existence in effect, the aspect of the Spirit will remain unchanged.

The second cited case infers definite aspects of change to the time existence of the Spirit. Here continuity of existence is by transfer and not by direct continuance as in the previous case. Since the Spirit is now part of an open system, it is susceptible to outside influences and effects. Accordingly, if it happens to have a time coincidence wherein there is a time-matching of one of its time points with that incurred in a moment of conception of a new life of the same species, then this spirit will form a partial imprint of itself upon the existence of the third dimensional group of this new life. When this life is born, this imprint of the Spirit will provide the basis of the second or closed memory. This second memory * references the behavior of the new life to provide the carry-over functions that are commonly referred to as instinct. As the new life senses the experiences of these induced behavior patterns, it adds this knowledge to the data that is continually being stored in the conventional or open memory. This conventional memory is located in the second dimensional group while the spirit imprint is located in the third dimensional group. Thus the imprint of the spirit is indirectly transferred to the new conventional memory section where, after the proper period of time required to obtain the necessary amount of data, the new Soul will be developed.

FOR A NEWBORN LIFE, THERE WILL BE A CONTINUITY OF SPIRIT DEVELOPED BY THE SPIRIT IMPRINT-TO-SOUL CONVERSION CAUSED THROUGH THE MECHANISM OF INDI-RECT TRANSFER FROM THE THIRD TO THE SECOND DIMENSIONAL GROUP.

By this method, the Soul to Spirit to Soul can continue almost indefinitely from life to new life. However, it must be

* See the book of LIFE

realized that the spirit imprint caused at a Moment of Conception is a composite activity which can cross family lines and which can involve more than just one spirit, if the time conditions are conducive. Thus the Spirit is altered as it moves down the line of lives. Depending upon the number of the spirits involved and what portion of each is used, each new composite Soul may be better or worse in accordance with the mix. In a sense, this seems to bear out the Hindu concepts which consider the aspects of a past life (Karma) coming in to affect a present life.

Due to the aspects of both cited means of Spirit operations, the effects of the Soul will continue indefinitely. If that which we call the Soul goes on and on, when and where did it begin? If we find ourselves in the midst of a process that is continuing, then it must have been going on well before the point where we decided to examine it. If this process continues indefinitely into the future, then it must have been going on indefinitely in the past. If the origin of the Soul goes way back in time, where does it begin?

Existence Theory (see the book of EXISTENCE) states that in an initial creation from a total condition of nothing, there can be one and only one first step. This is carefully and critically defined in mathematics. This step is exact and there can be no deviation whatsoever. This first step is the time point of creation and occurs mathematically right in the middle of the Life Range of existence. That this first point should be in the Life Range is considered to be most important. It is here that Life formally starts. From this point, all Life stems. From this one initial point, everything else comes to be.

Since this initial point represents the very first something in the Universe and since this first something is related to Life, this point is further related to the concept of God discussed in Chapter 6. Indeed, there is a quotation in the Bible (Colossians 1:15) that states ". . . God, the firstborn of every creature." This could be interpreted to place that which we call God in this very critical initial creation point. Since there are two pathways involved with the extensions of the Soul, and since qualities and characteristics have been identified which establish aspects of an infinite series and infinity with both pathways, and since no interruptions have been found in the process, it must be concluded that both pathways have their origin back at the first step or the initial point of creation.

The concept of the Soul, as the reference of Life operations, can be further considered with respect to some examples. A phonograph record player produces music when it operates. This music directly comes from the record that is being played. The particular record actually contains its own built-in musical patterns and thus is the reference for the phonograph. As this reference, the record can be said to be the "Soul" of this music producing system. This record or "Soul" is actually something which is separate and distinct from the composite of the main working mechanism and the included electronics. It could play or work with any composite phonograph mechanism, but any such mechanism must have a record before it can provide its musical function. Thus there can be no useful operation of the phonograph without the most important element—the record. In a similar fashion, there can be no useful operation of a physical presence of Life without its most important referencing element—the Soul.

In addition to referencing Life, the Soul also references the thinking process. The categories and the workings of the main elements of a digital computer (see Figure 2) can provide further comparisons to illustrate the previously described functionings of the multi-dimensional operations of the human thinking process. To present this, three separate GROUPS of multi-dimensions will be considered in the dual categorization that is shown in Figure 2. Here three sets of

125

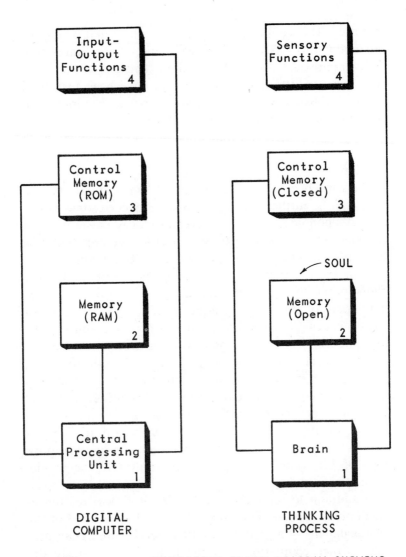

DIGITAL
COMPUTER

THINKING
PROCESS

FIGURE 2 - COMPARISON BLOCK DIAGRAM SHOWING
THE MAJOR SECTIONS OF A DIGITAL
COMPUTER ALONGSIDE THE SIMILAR
ASPECTS OF THE THINKING PROCESS.

126

pairs of similar functions will be examined and compared especially from the point of view that they are operating at three different locations.

All major data processing of the computer is performed in the particular section known as the "Central Processing Unit" (or CPU). This is analogous to the human thinking processing which is performed within the physical confines of the Brain. To facilitate this comparison, the CPU circuitry is placed on its own separate circuit board which is labelled "1" in the lower right hand corner of its representative box of the Comparison Block Diagram. For the Thinking Process, the Brain is considered to be in the FIRST Dimensional Group (of the physical presence) so that it too gets a "1" notation in the lower right hand corner of its representative box of the Comparison Block Diagram. In a like manner, the Random Access Memory (RAM) is placed on its own separate circuit board with notation "2," while the control memory or Read Only Memory (ROM) receives the notation "3" on its separate circuit board. In this way, each of the separate major computer functions is noted as operating in a different location.

This system of operations, whereby the computer performs its major functions in three separate locations, is similar to the dispersed functionings of the human thinking process. While the various sections of the computer are on three different circuit boards, similar sections of the human thinking process are each located in a different GROUP of dimensions included within the overall structure of the composite multi-dimensional geometry of the existent Universe. The Open Memory (or Soul) represents the extension of existence into the Second Dimensional Group of the physical presence of the Brain (in the First Dimensional Group). It should be remembered that a Group consists of a complete set of dimensions so that a suitable geometrical container is provided to hold the respective existence or portion thereof. To hold

127

the physical presence, the First Dimensional GROUP consists of the three conventional dimensions associated with Euclidean geometry.

The extension of existence of the Soul (or what we are calling herein the Open Memory) provides for the Third Group (which contains the Control or Closed Memory). Similar to the descriptive presentation of the Computer, the Human Thinking Process has its functions operating out of separated locations. Thus the thinking process is seen as a set of various functions centered in locations of different Groups of dimensions.

Now that the presence and origin of the Soul have been examined, it is important to consider the further operations and applications associated with the Soul. It has already been mentioned how a previous Soul in the aspect of the open Spirit can be latched onto at a moment of conception (if the associated time function points coincide) to provide for the Soul imprint to reference the personality of a new-born life. A Spirit can also latch onto and influence an operational Soul in a Life situation and cause unusual effects to that life.

In a closed operational life system, the included Soul is not usually susceptible to any outside effects. However, if there has been a general weakening of the associated life, and if a Spirit comes in proximity to the operational Soul, and if there is a similarity between the time functions of this operational Soul and the outside Spirit such that several time points coincide, then it is possible that there can be a merger of some of the respective portions of the outside Spirit into the operational Soul. If this should happen, there would be a definite change in some of the characteristics of the associated life. The personality would be subject to definite and very apparent change. One of the worst effects would be the incurring of the aspects of Sickness.

One of the greatest problems resulting from an inadvertent

inclusion of an outside Spirit into an operational Soul is the producing of undesirable interactions. Such interactions could manifest themselves back in the primary or first dimensional group as some sickness or disease in the physical presence. This adverse effect of an outside Spirit literally entering into an operational Soul can be responsible for a whole set of health problems that definitely will not respond to any regular type of medical or other usual forms of treatment.

Consider the following. There is an operational system of life which has a reasonably normal distribution of existence. This life has its distribution portion that can be identified with the concept of the Soul operating in the second dimensional group. This means that the human life involved in this analysis is over 12 years of age, and can be considered to be an adult. Operating also in the second dimensional group in proximity to the Soul, is a separate Spirit. In accordance with Time Theory, the life system in operation is referenced by time functions set at various time rates. This establishes the time rate associated with the included Soul. The separate Spirit has a similar time function operating at a similar time rate as compared to that of the mentioned Soul. With proximity in location and similarity in time, an inclusion is caused to happen wherein a portion of the Spirit enters into the operational domain of the mentioned Soul. Following this inclusion effect, interactions take place between the Spirit and the Soul. The results of these interactions are manifested in the physical presence in the conventional Euclidean 3-dimensional space. These manifestations are in the form of adverse health problems superimposed upon the subject life form. When these health problems are taken to a regular medical doctor, it is found that the included condition does not respond to conventional treatment.

These included health problems can take a variety of forms. Very often, the problem will be arbitrarily categorized

129

as being psychosomatic. However, this word is a total misnomer. For it will be neither of the mind (psycho) nor of the body (somatic). Actually, this type of problem has aspects that can be traced to the inclusions and interactions of an outside spirit.

If this outside Spirit was formally associated with a life system that had a particular and pronounced disease just prior to its death, the format and effects of that disease will have been entered and stored in the memory portion of the thinking process of this other life. For an adult human being, this memory portion is located in the second dimensional group which is in proximity to that which is called the Soul. If this Spirit should somehow come in contact with a Soul in an operational life system, then the associated interactions could cause a transfer of the included format and effects of this last disease, so that there could be a carry-over to the operational life system. The overall result would be that the disease or health problem would manifest itself in the physical presence of the operational life system.

Even the Bible has discussed the possibility that evil spirits are responsible for certain sicknesses. This is mentioned many times in various sections wherein miraculous cures, in certain cases, involve the driving out of spirits. "And certain women, which had been healed of evil spirits and infirmities, . . ." (Luke 8:2).

There can be many other manifestations resulting from the inclusion of an outside spirit. If these inclusions were only of temporary duration but repeating from reactions with the same outside Spirit, then the resulting changes in the physical presence would take on aspects that are currently considered as multiple personality. If the inclusions were only of a very partial nature, then there would still be distinct changes, but they would be categorized as "moodiness" rather than the much more pronounced aspects of multiple personality. In a very unusual situation where the former life associated

130

with the Spirit had severe mental health problems, a condition of short time duration might be transferred which would take on the irrational aspects of temporary insanity. The possible effects cited would be much more pronounced if the associated spirit was derived from a life system which had suffered a premature or sudden death. In any life system, each of the separate distributions of existence have prescribed intervals of time for their particular spans of existence. During these intervals, various particular happenings must take place. In the closed system where the subject life goes to reasonable completion (i.e.—dies at old age), all the necessary included happenings are synchronized to occur with each other. However, in an open system where the subject life dies prematurely (i.e.—accident, disease, etc.) the intermediate happenings that were not fulfilled, must still take place. But now these happening functions are open ended wherein they are relatively free to influence outside situations. These Spirits associated with a prematurely ended life have a very high propensity to influence operational Souls in a closed or full existing life system. In fact, the time of highest influence would occur at the time point of one of these open-ended happening functions.

The Soul is the reference and the most critical portion of life. The Soul begins as a Spirit imprint at the moment of conception. It is formed at two geometrical dimensional positions back from the physical presence. In this third dimensional group it is protected from the many devastating problems associated with the physical presence in the first dimensional group.

At the moment of birth, we find that there are three sets of existences, each appearing separately. The first is the physical presence. The second is the conventional memory of the human thinking process which is relatively empty at this time. In the third dimensional group is the imprint of the Spirit whose time functions and time points coincide at the moment of conception. During its initial stages, the newborn life is being referenced by the imprinted Spirit functioning in the third dimensional existence group. Thus the result is a set of predetermined behavior patterns which are then performed by the physical presence. These are usually and nebulously attributed to the category of instinct.

The performance of the different behavior patterns become experiences which can be absorbed by the newborn life and then inserted into its newly beginning conventional memory. Thus this conventional memory slowly and continually acquires more and more of the reference information contained in the imprint. There is a transfer involved, but it is accomplished by an indirect process. As the conventional memory is building up its quantity of stored data, the imprinted memory is slowly fading. Up until the age of six for a human being, the imprinted Spirit memory is the dominant reference. After the age of twelve, the conventional memory becomes dominant. Thus we can define the concept of child and adult in terms of the associated dimensional dominance. The life of a child is always referenced by the third dimensional group. An adult can be defined as always being referenced by the second dimensional group.

When the physical presence terminates or dies, the existences in the other dimensional groups still continue but on a less controlled or open basis. The open Soul has much less constraint upon it and, in this freer condition, becomes known as a Spirit. In this condition, the Spirit can sometimes interact with Souls of operational life systems, wherein problems can be created.

Since concepts of both Time Theory and Existence Theory have been used to derive the various aspects discussed concerning the Soul, knowledges of both these concepts will be important in dealing with the various associated problems.

12

THE SOUL OF GOD

"But God hath revealed them unto us by his Spirit:
for the Spirit searcheth all things,
yea, the deep things of God."
(The Bible, N.T., 1 Corinthians 2:10)

When we consider the Deity, we often tend to think of Him just in terms of His being "God." For God is the ultimate being. His work is beyond question. His accomplishments are most apparent. His Universe is awe inspiring and huge beyond all imagination. Yet with all this, there is still so much more to God.

One of the more obscure aspects of God in the subject of His totality of being. For this being includes various multiple aspects. And these have identification in both the existent Universe and in the non-existent Realm of Nothing.

One of the most direct and useful methods of descriptive approach is to invoke the conjugate pair of the noumenon-phenomenon relationship. The definition of this conjugate pair is that the noumenon represents what the subject actu-

133

ally IS while the phenomenon represents what the subject actually DOES.

It is important to note that a phenomenon can only take place in the existent Universe. A phenomenon represents a happening which is the result of an operation or a functioning. Since there is nothing in the Realm of Nothing, no operations and thus no phenomena can take place there.

In direct contrast, the noumenon is usually separated from its associated phenomenon. What the something is, is usually apart from the results that the something causes. Thus the start or the cause of a happening is often at a location other than where the results or the happening take place.

The manifestation of God in the existent Universe represents a phenomenon. The reference of God has been identified as being located in the non-existent Realm of Nothing. This reference represents what God is and, as such, is the noumenon of God. Since the Soul is defined as being the reference of Life and containing the various aspects and major qualities, the noumenon of God is further identified as being the Soul of God.

Thus the Soul of God lies in the Realm of Nothing. This is especially fitting. Just as the non-existent Realm of Nothing is the necessary prelude and reference to the existent Universe, so is the Soul of God the necessary prelude and reference to all the Theological aspects and operations in the existent Universe.

As the reference, the Soul of God is especially important for preserving the continuity of the Theological Presence BEFORE and AFTER the manifestation of the existent Universe. The Time and the Existence relationships indicate that the existent Universe is cyclical in its being (see Chapter 23 herein). Not only does the Universe undergo a Creation, but it is (or will be) subject to a Termination. After Termination, the entire Universe will cease to be and all that will be left will be the Realm of Nothing. However, some time after

Termination when the proper conditions become present again, there will be another Creation. Being cyclical on a non-uniform time basis, this becomes a continually repeating process. Thus the Universe will exist during certain time periods and will be absent during others.

By definition, there can be no existence of any kind when the Universe (or at least some portion thereof) is not availble. Accordingly, between the periods of Existence, there will be gaps of Non-Existence. For the Theological perpetuation of God, it is absolutely essential that some means be available to allow for this requirement during the time gaps of Non-Existence. The concept of the Soul of God allows for this perpetuation requirement.

Of all the many aspects of the Soul of God, perhaps the most significant is the requirement to reference all religious Theology. For God to function, all His operations must be referenced and have some meaningful forms of organization. This referencing and direction are provided by the Soul of God.

In its noumenon capacity, the Soul of God is well suited to perform its referencing functions. Due to its location in the Realm of Nothing, nothing can affect it. It is in the most stable of positions. As such, it is relatively isolated and protected from outside influences. This is as it must be. For the referencing provided by the Soul of God must be the ultimate of all concepts and operations.

The question must now be asked—How does this Soul of God acquire its qualities and become the ultimate of all references? What provides this capability and insures its continuance?

The referencing aspect of the Soul of God derives its inherent capability from its association with the concept of Time. For Time has certain unique characteristics that can be used for the practical initiation of all possible operations. And the coordinating aspects of Time allow it to function in all the dimensions of the existent Universe as well as in the Realm of Nothing.

The identification and the comparison of God with Time has already been discussed herein (first in outline form in Chapter 3 and then in more detail in Chapter 10). It was presented that the Soul of God and the noumenon of Time are the only identifiable things in the Realm of Nothing. It was further noted that God has actually only two sets of powers and that these are identical with the only two capabilities of Time, which are Initiation and Termination. From these various comparisons and similar identifications, the theoretical Soul of God is considered to be identical to the practical concept involved with the noumenon of Time.

Therefore, when we worship or venerate God, we are actually dealing with and referring to the Soul of God which is located in the non-existent Realm of Nothing. When we talk about His work or His presence, we are dealing with the manifestations of God which can only occur in the existent Universe. From comparisons of theoretical Theology with a number of the practical considerations of Science, the Soul of God is concluded to be synonymous with the Physics concept of the noumenon of Time.

13

HEAVEN–THE REPOSITORY OF GOD

"Our Father which art in heaven,"
(The Bible, N.T., Matthew 6:9)

The beginning of the Lord's Prayer states that God is in heaven. But exactly what is meant by the term "heaven"? And where would this "heaven" be located?

Most Religions consider that there is a place where their God or Gods reside. Such a location has various different names depending upon the associated Religion. For example, Judaism and Christianity use the name of heaven. Islam uses "paradise." Ancient Greek mythology used Mount Olympus. Often this location of God is also associated with the final or desired resting place of the remnants of life or the Souls whose respective previous lives were involved with acts of goodness. Thus it is possible for heaven to take on an even more extensive meaning.

Since nothing existed before the Creation of the existent Universe, that which became known as heaven had to have its occurrence take place after this monumental event. As a further result of the Creation, it can be said that God began to develop a complete existence in which to manifest Himself. Each existence involves geometry and must begin from a point from which it will be said to emanate and evolve. To provide for that special existence of the manifestation of the phenomenon of God, there must also be a point of reference. Prior to the Creation, there was only an "identification" of God in the Realm of Nothing. With the event of Creation which brings about the manifestation of the existence of God, there is a requirement for a place to be associated with that existence. The place of existence for God is that which is called "heaven" (which will be the reference generic term used herein).

Heaven is mentioned in the very first part of The Bible where it is stated—

"In the beginning God created the heaven and the earth."

(Genesis 1:1)

This implies that the act of Creation involves the Theological origination of two things, which include the material Universe (or Earth) and the working location (or the repository) of God. Since Creation pertains only to the existent Universe, then that which is known as heaven is inferred to be in the existent Universe.

When The Bible presents heaven in association with the earth, the result is a duality of concepts. This combination of heaven and earth is used to completely include and categorize the entire existent Universe by dividing it into two parts. Thus we have the earth which represents that portion of the Universe that is identifiable through the senses, while the heaven refers to the Theological repository of God which is only identifiable through the mind. This allows the earth to represent the material Universe which then can be considered as "sensible" or perceptible to the senses. In contrast, heaven then is "intelligible" or discernible to the intellect.

It is especially fitting to consider heaven as an intelligible concept. The most important attribute of God (see Chapter 10) has been concluded to be the capability for organized thinking which, in its advanced form, becomes the basis for wisdom. God can be perceived as a center for thinking. Heaven, as the repository of God, can be perceived as facilitating the thinking activity by providing for the location of the thinking center.

Since Heaven is associated with God, the location of Heaven involves the location of God. But God can be identified as being in two places. The phenomenon of God is in the existent Universe, while the noumenon or Soul of God is located in the non-existent Realm of Nothing. Since Heaven is defined as being the location of God, it takes on a dualistic meaning wherein it must include and allow for both the noumenon (Soul) and the phenomenon (physical or existent manifestation) aspects.

Any phenomenon can be said to be an extension of the associated noumenon. Creation initiates the process that allows for the manifestation of the phenomenon. Just after Creation, the very first thing that is developed is the extension of the Soul of God. Thus the First Creation in the existent Universe is the existent God. The place of this First Creation is the location of heaven.

This First Creation, which is the first happening associated with the Creation of the Universe, takes place as an extension of the Realm of Nothing. The Realm of Nothing can actually be represented by a non-existent point beyond (and within) which, there is also nothing. When Creation begins, it does so with the non-existent point of Nothing as the geometric reference. It is the extension of this point in itself which forms the first location or place of existence in the newly emerging existent Universe.

The First Creation occurs at the first point or identifiable geometric place of existence that begins the existent Universe. This point is located in the first geometric dimension of the Universe and forms the pivotal point of all existence. With this point as reference or center, it is from here that everything else can be said to emanate. Thus this becomes the starting point as well as the geometric reference for the entire existent Universe.

When it is said that everything stems from God, it can also be said that all geometry in the existent Universe is referenced by heaven. This means that all dimensions and groups of dimensions have heaven as their reference or center point. As this reference point, heaven becomes a place of zero dimension. Thus as the dual repository of God, the heaven of the existent Universe and the heaven of the non-existent Realm of Nothing both are placed at the same point and both involve the situation of zero dimension.

The duality of heaven in both the domains of existence (the Universe) and non-existence (Realm of Nothing) allows for the continuity of God regardless of the condition of cyclical existence. Just as God must have continuity, so must His geometrical referencing also have such continuity. The duality of the location of heaven provides for this necessary attribute.

With heaven as the starting or focal point, all geometrical activity is referenced away and through the multi-dimensions as they develop. This starting point takes on additional significance as the reference center of all geometric operations of the Universe. As the existent Universe develops, this process is facilitated in the co-developing associated multi-dimensions.

The pivot point or the focal point for all geometric operations in the existent Universe is the heaven point of the First Creation. So critical is this point to the geometrical arrangement of the Universe, that if this point were to disappear or otherwise be unavailable, the entire structure of the Universe would be compromised with the result that all existence would stop and all associated operations and entities would then cease to be. THEREFORE HEAVEN, INSTEAD OF BEING JUST A PARADISE OF THEOLOGY, REPRE-SENTS A NECESSARY GEOMETRICAL REQUIRE-MENT OF GOD FOR THE MAINTENANCE AND CONTINUITY OF THE ENTIRE EXISTENT UNI-VERSE.

In perspective, that which is called heaven has a number of unusual attributes and characteristics. Primarily, heaven represents a geometrical location. In Theology, the most significant aspect of heaven is that it is the location of God. As such, it is a treasured place that represents everything that is considered to be beautiful, wonderful, desirable, and good. But beyond this aesthetical symbolism, it takes on a number of additional aspects in Theology.

As the reference location of the repository of the Soul as well as the manifestation of God, heaven is also associated with the geometrical facets of all the operations of God. Since the most significant aspect of the existent Universe is its included geometry, heaven incurs especial importance as the associated reference and focal point. All operations and happenings of the existent Universe must occur through the included geometry. Thus heaven becomes the means for implementing and geometrically referencing all of the Theological operations and the dictates of God.

Part IV

GOD AND MAN

14

MAIN THEOLOGICAL REASON FOR THE CREATION OF THE UNIVERSE

"Wisdom is the principal thing; therefore get wisdom: and with all thy getting get understanding."
(The Bible, O.T., Proverbs 4:7)

Why did God create the Universe? What is the main benefit of the Universe to God? What primary capability does the Universe provide for God? We shall now examine the question of—What is the major Theological Reason for the creation of the Universe?

Of all the questions in Theology, those dealing with the Theological Reasons for the Creation are considered to be among the most significant, the most startling, the most dramatic, and the most important of everything that can be asked. For in Theology, everything has a reason for being. Certainly that which is known as the Universe must also have such a reason for its being. And the being of this Universe must serve some definite purpose for God. Otherwise there would have been no need for its existence.

To consider this Theological Reason, we must first understand what was actually created when it is said that the Universe was created. And then within this understanding, we must determine what is the primary attribute or special feature of the Universe that takes priority in the forming of the Theological Reason.

The subject of the Creation of the Universe (and its associated aspects) has been examined separately, by the author, in each of the concurrent books on Physics, Time, and Existence. It has been shown from a Physics point of view that this Creation involved a process that was initiated by a time function (Time Theory) which, in turn, caused many sets of things to come into being (Existence Theory). The sum total of the effect of these many various existences resulted in that composite situation known as the Universe.

It is important to realize that once these existences are created, they must be shaped, positioned, held, and contained. Indeed, when the Universe is considered as a subject for study, often these geometrical aspects are usually neglected or omitted entirely. Yet in order to create anything, it is necessary to provide a place or a container to hold that which is created.

Truly the containing of the Universe is a tremendous task. It requires the very largest of all possible containers. It is literally and virtually an infinite container since it must contain everything that is or ever will be.

In contrast with this huge geometric structure is the relatively tiny amount of what is actually being contained within. This contained material represents the substance of the Universe. It is this substance material which is either directly called out or implied, whenever anyone talks about the existent Universe.

If the totality of all the substance in the Universe is compared to the huge size of the overall container of the Universe, an unusual conclusion becomes apparent. The overwhelmingly huge size of the container actually dwarfs the totality of everything that is included or held within.

The relationship of the occupied size of the total substance material compared to the total size (or container) of the Universe, can be expressed as a mathematical ratio. This ratio specifically tells how much of the existent Universe is actually filled. It tells, on a relative basis, how much of anything is really in the Universe. Since this is a mathematical relationship, it can be examined and tested mathematically. Now something quite unusual occurs. When various standard mathematical tests are applied to this substance-to-container ratio, the result is always the same. This ratio always approaches the value of zero as its limit and final answer. Since this ratio represents what is really in the Universe, the associated conclusion can be stated as follows:

FOR ALL PRACTICAL PURPOSES, THE UNIVERSE IS ACTUALLY EMPTY AND DEVOID OF ANY SUBSTANCE.

But if everything is empty and nothing actually exists in the Universe, then what has it to do with the Theological Reason? Why was this Universe created? And what purpose can it serve to God?

At this point with the information that we have just developed, we can eliminate one important possibility. If the totality of the substance of the Universe represents zero for all practical purposes, then the substance of the Universe can NOT be part of the major Theological Reason which we are seeking.

Although the substance of the Universe can be considered as being zero for all practical purposes, there is a relatively small amount of some substance that actually exists. A spe-

147

cial examination of this actual substance can be made from a theoretical point of view.

The actual substance of the Universe can be considered as including LIFE as well as the other categories of Matter and Energy. Among many other things, the category of Life includes mankind. By the elimination of the possibility of the substance of the Universe from further consideration in connection with the Theological Reason, we also eliminate any possibility of mankind having any prime connection with the Theological Reason as well. No matter what argument is presented to the contrary, the Creation of the Universe was just not done either because of, nor for, any reason connected with mankind. Thus for whatever purpose mankind may serve in the Theological order of things, mankind is definitely not part of the major Theological Reason for the creation of the Universe.

If the substance of the Universe is insignificant, and if the insignificant aspects do not have any substantial effect upon the Theological reason, then some significant aspect must be the major determining factor. The question thus becomes— When the Universe is created, what is the most significant aspect of this creation?

With respect to its almost infinite size, the most significant aspect of the Universe is its container. This container of the Universe can be described in the geometric terms of dimensions and dimensional groups. Each dimension provides for one individual boundary of the container. Sets or groups of dimensions provide particular enclosing capabilities within the overall holding framework. Since many such individual enclosing capabilities are possible, there is a propensity to develop numerous separate shapes within the different dimensional sets. This results in the aspect of containers within containers. In turn, this leads to the concept of the multidimensional Universe.

This geometric composite structure of countless dimensions within the container, references the scientific theory of the infinite dimensional Universe. Thus the container of the Universe is marked as being composed of a huge complex set of structures within other structures on an almost endless continuing scale. FROM A PHYSICS AND SCIENCE POINT OF VIEW, THIS COMPOSITE GEOMETRICAL REPRESENTATION DEPICTS A TREMENDOUS OVERALL STRUCTURAL ARRANGEMENT WHICH IS THE MOST SIGNIFICANT CHARACTERISTIC OF THE UNIVERSE.

The operations of the Universe must take place within this overall structure. The various elements involved in these operations often are situated in different dimensional locations. This requires that any necessary transferences or interchanges occur on an inter-dimensional basis. Of the many different types of operations associated with this inter-dimensional activity, the most important involves the functioning of the thinking process. Indeed, the completion of each and every thought cycle necessitates repeating operations that take place on a most definite multi-dimensional basis.

With all the foregoing in mind, let us itemize and list the various major aspects of the container with respect to the Universe. Accordingly, this container is considered to be significant due to the following reasons:

1. It provides the primary necessary function of containing the Universe.
2. It provides for the geometrical shape of each of the many individual existences within the Universe.
3. It references the having of containers within containers and thus provides for multiple dimensions.
4. It allows for all existence including multiple existence, separation of existence, and the extension and distribution of existence.
5. It allows for the existence of God.

6. Through the interchange between associated existences in different dimensions (or dimensional groups), it allows for the operation and functioning of a thinking process.

Now let us examine these aspects in relation to God and His associated requirements. Especially let us note which aspects are necessary for the functioning of God. For it is the necessity of the practical functioning of God that will be seen as the primary Theological Reason for the creation of the Universe.

One of the more important aspects of God is that He must have an operational identification both within and outside of the existent Universe. But in the outside non-existent Realm of Nothing, the operations of God are severely limited. Indeed, within the Realm of Nothing, God has only one capability or power, which is that of initiation and nothing else. With this in mind, it is important to realize that the full powers and capabilities of God can only be manifested and developed in the existent Universe. It is only here that things actually can be said to exist.

With respect to the previous list and the priority needs of God, the characteristics of shape and of being contained are not primary considerations (thereby eliminating listed Items 1, 2, and 3). As a means for implementing the formal existence of the Universe, the container represents a required initial condition. It is likened to the necessary firm road-bed for the tracks of a railroad train, but it is not the train itself. In this chapter, we are looking for the most important primary requirement for the Theological Reason for the creation of the Universe.

The capability of God to manifest His powers is another important possibility that should be examined herein. Influence could not be exerted nor power manifested by God and directed toward a particular subject or target unless there was some capability of concurrent existence within the selected location. Yet it should not be a primary Theological necessity to create an existence or an existent Universe just for the purpose of manifesting power. Thus the creation of a Universe just to allow for existence, even the existence of God, would also not be a candidate for the major Theological Reason (thereby eliminating Items 4 and 5). ONE OF THE MOST IMPORTANT OF ALL THE QUALITIES OF GOD IS THAT HE MUST HAVE AND EXERCISE TREMENDOUS WISDOM. But to facilitate the dispensing of wisdom, there must first be a capability for a thinking process. For a thinking process to function, there is a mandatory requirement for an associated environment consisting of a set of existing multiple separate geometrical dimensional groups. It has been determined (see the book of LIFE) that at least two individual geometrical dimensional groups are required before that which is known as thinking can ever become functional. Whatever else may otherwise be presented or considered, there is just no capability or possibility for any of the necessary structuring of the required sets of dimensions or dimensional groups to take place outside of the existent Universe. Dimensional structuring is an attribute of existence that can only occur in an existent Universe.

Since thinking is a functional process that is dependent upon the existence of geometrical dimensions, it would be totally impossible to achieve unless there is an existent Universe. For God to function properly, He must have the capability to think. The Physics of this situation is most definite. Without a Universe and its inherent multiple geometrical dimensions, the process of thinking just can not be performed. THEREFORE, TO PROVIDE GOD WITH THE CAPABILITY OF THINKING, THE UNIVERSE MUST BE CREATED.

The Theological Reason for the creation of the Universe is

considered to be an ego actuated reason initiated by God. The situation prior to Creation is a unique one. There is no Universe. There is nothing else except the Realm of Nothing (or Zero). There is nothing outside of this Realm of Nothing. There is no space, nor empty vastness, nor geometrical structure of any kind. Especially there are no dimensions. Without geometrical dimensional groups, there can be no capability for thinking.

For God to function and to realize self-actualization, He must attain thinking and ultimately wisdom. This can only be achieved if there is a set of dimensions. Such dimensions only occur and only can be derived in an existent Universe. Therefore it is necessary for God to have a Universe. Accordingly, the main Theological Reason for the Creation of the Universe is to provide for God the means to attain this thinking capability.

With respect to the manifestation and the functioning of God, it is important to understand what was actually involved and happening during the occurrence of the existent Universe after its Creation. At the Beginning, there was Nothing. This meant that there were none of the necessary conditions or background environment available to support the process of thinking. There was just no possibility whatsoever to indulge in or to produce thinking in any form by anything or anyone. This priority situation can even be applied to God.

This overall situation with its inherent inability to support thinking is especially significant in the Realm of Nothing. Here in this Domain of Zero, nothing exists by definition. Thus the desired operation of thinking becomes a distinct impossibility.

After the Creation of the Universe, this situation could not change immediately. All functionings of every type and description, were tied and linked to corresponding developments that were taking place in the evolving Universe.

152

Nothing could occur before its Time. During its Beginning, the existent Universe was being developed in its early stages by *definition*, and not by any outside control. Without the full powers of thinking capability, God was in no position to actively provide any control.

In any analysis of sequential mathematical or serial functions such as those involved in the thinking process and the development of the existent Universe, there are three very special points that take priority of precedence over all other possible considerations. These make up the Tri-Point Concept and include the Sex Point, the Wisdom Point, and the Termination Point. Specifically, these have their foundations in the E-L-M Tabulations of existence and particularly refer to the most significant mathematical ratios or proportions involved in general serial functions. This Tri-Point Concept includes the following proportions:

TRI-POINT NAMES	PROPORTION
Sex Point	1/8
Wisdom Point	1/2
Termination Point (Phase-Out Point)	7/8

CHART 1 - PROPORTIONS OF THE TRI-POINT CONCEPT

For the development of the thinking process, the proportion "1/8" known as the "Sex Point," * is also called the "Thinking Point." It is associated with the attainment of the mental situation known as "Maturity." Maturity is defined as taking place when the included thinking process starts to produce useful results on a relatively continuous basis. Mature thinking can not just come about immediately. Even for God, a certain amount of Time must pass to allow the transition from the state of zero thinking (in the Realm of Nothing) to the achievement of the capability for the organized thinking required for maturity in the existent Universe.

During this transition period (the first 1/8 of the total), thinking exhibits the unorganized and often random qualities of immaturity. But even after reaching the condition of maturity, it still takes quite an additional amount of Time to reach the ultimately desired capability for Wisdom.

The capability for Wisdom is said to be attained when the continuing development of the thinking process reaches the Wisdom Point. The Wisdom Point is considered to be at the exact center (or half-way) along the mathematical series function associated with the thinking process.

The concept that is being stated here is this. Nothing changes instantaneously! The conditions necessary to facilitate thinking take time to come into being. This holds for any new-born life (or even God) and requires a minimum of 1/8 of whatever the total time period involved. This relates to the total Universe or anything else that can be compared and likened as a universe in itself. Each form of Life can be considered as a smaller scale version of the universe. But God can only be compared to the full Universe where the development of His manifestation will directly correspond to the actual developments of this totality of existence. These

* (named in accordance with the research in which it was first discovered, dealt with in the chapter entitled "Derivation of Sex" in the book of LIFE)

154

developments, especially in their early stages, proceeded by definition and certainly not by any thinking control. Thus thinking was not involved in the control of the development of the Universe. Rather the development of the existent Universe was required to facilitate the thinking process of God!

As the development of the Universe continued, its ever increasing composite of contents produced the necessary conditions required to facilitate thinking. This continuing development provided increasing numbers of these various conditions, which are mathematically described in detail by the Concepts of the Steps and the Points (see Chapters 23 and 24). When this development reached the half-way point, then and only then were the resulting conditions sufficient to allow for that capability known as Wisdom to occur.

The most important quality or attribute of God is considered to be Wisdom. The conditions that allow for thinking and eventually wisdom, are never available in the Realm of Nothing. These conditions can only occur in the existent Universe, and then only after particular time periods of development (1/8 for the start of organized thinking, and 1/2 for the beginning of wisdom). The most significant conditions required to permit thinking involve the geometrical structure of multi-dimensions, which are only found in the existent Universe. To provide for thinking, there must be a Universe. Therefore, the main Theological Reason for the Creation of the Universe is to provide God with the environment and the conditions that allow for the capability of thinking, and ultimately Wisdom.

15

OTHER THEOLOGICAL REASONS FOR THE EXISTENCE OF THE UNIVERSE

"But the manifestation of the Spirit is given to every man to profit withal."
(The Bible, N.T., 1 Corinthians 12:7)

It is said that there is a Universe and that this Universe exists and continues to exist. Yet why should this be so? What Theological reasons does this existence serve?

Since reasons can be found or considered for everything, there must be Theological reasons for the continued existence of the Universe. In Theology, it is said that all things emanate from God. In addition, it can be further said that all things are for God. Thus the Theological reasons for the continued existence of the Universe would be primarily to meet and serve the requirements and other associated aspects of God.

It was ascertained that the primary reason for the Creation of the Universe was to provide God with the capability for thinking, so that this would ultimately lead to that which is called wisdom. This was facilitated through the development of the geometric dimensions which represent the single most significant characteristic of the Universe.

The geometric dimensions can be said to form the container of the Universe. Within this container are the contents or the substance of the Universe (Energy, Life, and Matter) which also provide Theological capabilities to God. If the abstract aspects of the dimensions facilitate the capability for thinking, then it is the physical aspects associated with the substance that can implement the physical results of that thinking. Thus it is this substance that can serve God by allowing for His presence and His functioning within the existent Universe.

The substance of the Universe consists of the three major categories of Energy (E), Life (L), and Matter (M). Of these, Matter can be considered as being most closely associated with the form geometry and dimensions of the Universe. Energy is most associated with the operations and the functioning of the Universe. It is left mostly to the category of Life to provide for the manifestation of God and the implementation of His powers.

Life is especially suited to provide for the phenomenon of God. It is Life which gives the animated qualities to the various portions of the Universe. IT IS ONLY LIFE WHICH CAN ALLOW FOR POSSIBLE DEVIATIONS IN THE OPERATIONS OF THE UNIVERSE. For Energy and Matter are bound inexorably to the prescribed dictates of Predestination in the mandatory order and the sequential operations included and required in the Universe.

However, the category known as Life has certain inherent capabilities that can permit deviations to the predetermined order of things. These deviations can be exercised through the decision making ability that is associated with a developed thinking process. Only Life has this capacity for thinking. The more advanced and the more complex the Life-form, the more advanced and the more complex will be the associated capacity for thinking.

This concept which involves the deliberate deviation away from the fixed and prescribed dictates of the Universe, is known as "Free Will." From a mechanistic or operations concept, Free Will can be further described as the intentional reshuffling of the operations or task possibilities noted by the set of representative mathematical points (P) located between each ordered step (S) in the predetermined sequential operations which are required to facilitate the existence of the Universe (see Chapter 23).

The thinking process is the primary example of specifically deviating the occurrence order of the points (relating to the tasks) that take place between the steps of existence. It is by the process of thinking that the basis is established for any initial idea or desire. As the thinking is continued, it offers the means by which an idea is implemented. Whatever the consequences may finally be, it is the included attempts at organized thinking that are mostly responsible for the associated results.

For Theology, thinking represents the most important of all activities. It is the most important single attribute of God. It is thinking that gives everything meaning. It is thinking that establishes everything. It is thinking that has allowed for the Universe. It was because of the primary necessity to provide God with the capability of thinking that the Universe was created (see Chapter 14).

In essence, the Universe is what we think it is. All things are ultimately what they are assessed at being. In considering existence, anything is or is said to be, by virtue of its meeting the definition of its own existence (see the book of EXISTENCE). And it is thinking which evaluates and judges all the various assessments and definitions.

Especially, thinking is necessary to Religion. Indeed, all

158

Religions recognize in various ways, the importance of thinking. Some of these, like Hinduism and Zen Buddhism, elevate aspects of thinking to the very highest levels. They give it top priority, and make it mandatory that their adherents do extra and specified thinking (and related aspects thereof) in the form of meditation. Often, they even go well beyond this. They present to their followers a whole new perspective on the Universe and everything in it. Various requirements in different forms are made so that an understanding of life, existence, purpose, and meaning can be developed. Such an understanding can only be arrived at and experienced through the demanding rigors of specially organized thinking as specified in the dictates, rules, and dogma of the particular Religion.

Thinking, the most important attribute of God, is also present and developed in the more advanced forms of Life. With respect to this thinking capability, this means that for God, there is an extension of His being into these advanced Life-forms. Mankind is at the extreme end of this chain of advanced Life so that Man represents the ultimate or final extension of God. Indeed this concept is a definite part of the Theology of certain Religions. In Zen Buddhism, each person is considered to be endowed with the potential capability of Buddhahood such that the qualities of the original leader, Gautama Buddha, are available to each and every true follower. In its huge polytheistic pantheon, Hinduism has an estimated number of Gods in the high millions, the total amount of which has been likened to the number of Hindu followers. In certain denominations embracing Christianity, it is believed that there is part of Jesus Christ in every one of the included followers. In the Judaic portion of the Holy Bible, it is stated in the Old Testament

(26) And God said, Let us make man in our image, after our likeness:—

(27) So God created man in his own image, in the image of God created he him; male and female created he them.

(Genesis 1:26, 27)

In this presented form, the inference is that the created man
has some of the qualities or characteristics associated with
the extension of God. Thus each person (in fact every form
of life for that matter) can be thought of as being a part of or
an extension of God.

If each form of life is an extension of God, then the ca-
pabilities and powers of each individual are then actually
available for the direct control, manipulation, and use by
God. This means that at any given time, God can be consid-
ered to be manifested in any one or more forms of life.
THUS IT BECOMES POSSIBLE IN BOTH THE FIGUR-
ATIVE AND THE LITERAL SENSE, FOR GOD TO AP-
PEAR IN ANY FORM OF LIFE INCLUDING HUMAN.
This bears out such concepts as the avatar in Hinduism, or
the incarnation of Jesus in Christianity as the Son of God.

Thus God has the means of exercising His will through the
use of the powers and the capabilities of any Life-form, or
any combination of Life-forms so as to produce the condition—

"Thy will be done in earth, as it is in heaven."

(Matthew 6:10)

In addition to the concept of God extended into all life,
the reverse is also true. All life in the Universe can be related
back to the origin or fountainhead, which is God (see Chapter 6). One of the means of developing this relationship is to
go back through the dimensions using concepts associated
with the Soul (see Chapter 11). This allows life of all types to
be traceable back to God. Thus it can be said that all actions

and associated happenings of each Life-form can be considered as being initiated and inspired by God.

God therefore becomes the referencing so that all activities of each and every Life-form can be interpreted as being acts by God to implement His will. Thus it is through the category of Life that God manifests Himself and exercises His powers.

The rest of the contents of the Universe provide for the remaining requirements and other associated aspects of God. If God is to manifest Himself, He must be able to do this at a particular somewhere. The Universe with its geometry of dimensions, allows for this capability. If God is to have powers, these must be referenced to something. This something is Matter which is available in its innumerable forms which have their various extensions appearing in the many dimensions. The consequences of powers are effected through various happenings, events, entities, and operations. The producing, maintaining, and changing of all these requires Energy. Thus it is that the effects of Energy, Life, and Matter are accounted for. It can be said that the totality of the existent Universe is for the expressed purpose of providing for the requirements of the phenomenon of God.

But Energy (E), Life (L), and Matter (M) are subject to the specific laws and definitions of Existence. They are bound and must follow the fixed relationships defined by the ordered sequential Steps of Creation and by the E-L-M Tabulations called out and noted in Existence Theory. Thus the manifestation of the Phenomenon of God in the existent Universe is regulated by the laws and the requirements of Existence.

Once the Creation of the Universe is initiated, the steps of existence development are precisely ordered and regulated by the requirements of Existence Theory. However, between these steps, independent deviations can occur in the times in which the included tasks and happenings take place. Thus

161

the Predestination specified by Existence Theory can be modified somewhat by certain small variations in Time Theory. It is these variations in Time Theory that allow for that which is called Free Will.

From all this, a new overall picture begins to emerge for the cosmos of existence. It is a composite of predetermined order (Existence Theory) with free will type variations (Time Theory) which is the repository for the manifestation of the phenomenon of God (Theology Theory). Thus it is that the existence of the Universe provides for the operational cycle of the ego-representation of God.

16

THE RELATIONSHIP OF MAN TO GOD

"I am thy chosen one from the very beginning."

(Zoroastrian Avesta)

All scriptures of all major religions reserve very special considerations for the relationship of man to God. Indeed, it is often inferred that in his worship of God, man is the chosen form of life, enjoying special position in the Theological hierarchy of things. Here this included order of Life places man very high in the hierarchy, well above all the so-called lesser animals.

As Life developed in the Universe, the various included forms became arranged into a predetermined order. First came the very simplest forms of Life. As more developed in the Universe, there was a greater selection in terms of the available basic building blocks. With more available, each new Life form could become more complex than its predecessors. Thus in the developing Universe, there is found an included hierarchy of Life forms in a specific order of continually increasing complexity.

Within this hierarchy, man is a very advanced and highly complex form of Life. Indeed man is at the extreme end of this Life chain. At this end of the order, there is a special characteristic that can be identified with the associated higher life forms. This characteristic involves the capability to think.

The capability to perform thinking is facilitated and enhanced as the complexity of the Life-form is increased. Of all the attributes of mankind, the most important is considered to be this capability for advanced thinking. This is especially so from the philosophical point of view. Many philosophers believe that the entire biological structure of man is for just one purpose — to support and maintain the brain and its thinking operations. Indeed, the definition of the word *man* is believed to have come from the Latin *mens* which means *the mind.* Thus man, in its basic sense, implies that form of Life that thinks. And it is this unique capability for advanced thinking that makes man so very useful for providing the Theological operations of God.

In contrast to the possibility of advanced thinking at the complex end of the ordered Life spectrum, there is no such capability present at the other end. This leads us into an important major concept that involves the Life positional placements in the relationship of Man to God. In the general hierarchy of the Theological order of Life, God and Man appear at the opposite extremes of the included tabulation. The Theological order starts off with God in the very first position. This represents the simplest form. With this as a beginning, the hierarchy of Life continues onward. As the series continues, the various types of Life increase in complexity as the order advances. Finally Man as a highly advanced form of Life appears on the complex side of this

Theological hierarchy. Herein lies a very serious and unexpected consideration.

In the Theological order of Life (as well as everything else), God must precede everything else and therefore appears first (in the Alpha position). Man appears at the advanced Life end (in the Omega position). In this arrangement, Man would seem to be more advanced and more complex than God. Yet it is God who must be the most advanced and most complex of all the forms of Life.

In dealing with this situation, a first clue for its interpretation comes from The Bible where it is stated —

"I am Alpha and Omega, the beginning and the end, the first and the last."

(Revelation 22:13)

From this statement, God would have to occupy BOTH positions. Since Man is in the Omega position, Man then becomes the actual extension of God in this very critical position.

Considering this possibility further, there is an additional quotation from the Bible that also appears to have a direct bearing upon this situation. This states —

"And God said unto Moses, I AM THAT I AM: and he said, Thus shalt thou say unto the children of Israel, I AM hath sent me unto you."

(Exodus 3:14)

It is this phrase "I AM" that is especially unique and that warrants extra attention. It appears in both of the cited quotations. In the first quotation, it is followed by "Alpha and Omega." In the second quotation, it is followed by "THAT I AM." It has already been established herein that

165

God is definitely synonymous with Alpha, and that Man is identified with the Omega position. In addition, the first Bible quotation links God with Omega, thereby linking and identifying Man with God. The second quotation, by its repeat of "I AM," places this phrase in the Omega position in the stated sequence. This identifies Man with the second "I AM." Thus it can be inferred from the Bible that Man represents the "I AM" of God.

That this is so can be seen from the contrasting positions of God and Man on the tabulation of the Life Range (or L-Tabulation of Existence). The needs of God are such that He should have been in the position or tabular location of Man from the point of view of required complexity and advanced operational placement. It is mandatory that God have this advanced position to function properly with complete capabilities. But Man occupies it. Therefore, God must perform His work through Man. This necessitates that Man becomes an extension of God.

The occupying of the two important positions of Alpha and Omega implies a further special relationship associated with God. The alpha is the key initial position. It represents the qualities and the main characteristics of God. It constitutes what God IS. As such, this Alpha or first position represents the NOUMENON of God (or what God is).

The Omega position is on the opposite end of the Life Range in the existent Universe. It is far more complex and is located in the realm of Man. With this position thus located, it is considered to be an important extension of God. By using this extension in the realm of Man, it permits God to perform His functions in the so-called real world. It is through this position that God manifests Himself using Man as His Instrument. This Omega position is characterized by the actions of God in the existent Universe. Thus it is constituted by what God DOES. As such, the Omega or final position represents the PHENOMENON of God (or what God does).

The phenomenon of God is therefore His manifestation in the real world or existent Universe. This manifestation or physical presence of God is represented by Man. It is Man who carries out the work of God. This then becomes the major relationship of Man to God, and the main Theological reason for the continued existence of Man.

As a further commentary, the noumenon of God represents the Soul of God. In contrast to the Omega position where Man becomes the physical extension of God,

THE ALPHA POSITION REPRESENTS
THE LOCATION OF THE SOUL OF GOD.

Since the Realm of Nothing is considered to be the actual repository of the Soul of God, the Alpha position is considered to be the extension of the Soul of God from the Realm of Nothing into the existent Universe.

17

OPERATIONAL ASPECTS OF MAN-MADE ORGANIZATIONS

"For as the body is one, and hath many members, and all the members of that one body, being many, are one body:"
(The Bible, N.T. 1 Corinthians 12:12)

One of the most important considerations of organized religion is that it involves the use of man-made organizations. The theory of religion can be examined and discussed in terms of the subject area of Theology. Theology is the study of God and associated religious concepts. In contrast, the so-called practical implementation of any religion requires that there be a large following of people. This is the man-made organization and, as the name implies, it is something created by man. God-made and man-made mark two very distinct and different sets of operations. So far, we have been considering Theological subjects. But the Theological must interface with man. Therefore it is important that we understand the included operational aspects of man-made organizations.

Man is a social creature and tends to usually combine himself with others to perform his work in group operations. Thus the man-made organization provides for the extension of the capabilities of man. In his pursuit of religion, it is logical that this too should be an organized effort. So it is. Like so many other grouping activities (i.e., Government, the Military, Businesses, Labor Unions, Schools, Hospitals, and Political Parties), the creation of any particular Religion requires the associated operations of the man-made organization. A following of large numbers of people is necessary to provide support and facilitate the continuance of the Religion and to promote mass faith in God. If these high purposes are to be achieved, all these people must be organized and directed in specific tasks and activities.

In their theoretical and practical operations, man-made organizations of every type and description must follow prescribed rules and concepts of the Universe. These aspects of organization are so definite that distinct order, conduct, and resultant effects can be identified with specific certainty. With these aspects providing a formalized basis, efficient standardized use can then be made of the administrational tools of examination, analysis, evaluation, critique, and interpretation. Many benefits can be obtained from the directed use of these tools. Accordingly, plans can be originated, strategies can be developed, selections instituted, policies formulated, decisions made, and appropriate actions taken for the purpose of achieving the desired results.

There is a special difference between man-made operations and those of the Universe. The Universe usually follows the exact dictates of Time Theory. Man, as a rational creature, tries to deliberately deviate from this process. Man insists upon having some set of reasons for everything that he does. Whether these reasons are actually so or not is usually of minor importance. Man must rationalize. Even the organized system of thinking that he most uses is tailor-made to fit this need. This thinking system is called Logic. It is man-made. It was created by man to meet the particular needs of his apparent world. And it does fulfill these particular needs.

The dominant feature of Logic is that it is a sequential process. It includes a series of steps wherein each step must be handled separately and completed before advancing to the next one. The major problem with Logic is that if any step can not be completed, the operations stop there and the entire process comes to a complete halt. Since Logic was created by man, it works on any kind of a problem in a subject category that was also created by man. Such subject categories include banking, inventory control, and the handling of credit cards. Conversely, it is usually not suited for the detailed processing of specific problems created in and by the Universe. One of the purposes of this book has been to show that the Universe does not operate in accordance with Logic-type principles.

Man-made organizations will differ from conventional aspects of the Universe mainly in the referencing of the included operations. Logic (or some form of it) references the man-made organizations. Time Theory (or some form of it) references the operations of the Universe. Logic, as well as its variations, is not natural to the Universe. It is artificial. It is something conceived and developed by man.

Due to certain aspects concerning their artificial creation, organizations tend to take on the attributes, characteristics, and life-style of man. Like man, an organization:

1. Is created.
2. Tends to grow.
3. Manifests a personality due to its policies.
4. Tries to perpetuate itself.
5. Tries to develop and maintain a position in the society.
6. Develops and exerts influence.

7. Requires and uses money, similar to the use of blood by man.
8. Maintains communication with its own elements as well as other organizations.
9. Exhibits variations in a cycle of existence.
10. Exhibits a displacement effect wherein it tends to displace (by its increasing presence) things in its immediate environment, natural operations by its operations, and other organizations.

The problem of unwieldy growth is common to all man-made organizations. Nothing can escape change (the phenomenon initiated by time). Due to the effects of change, an organization will either tend to decrease or increase in size. Unlike natural entities in the Universe, a man-made organization has no natural constraints or time-initiated regulatory operations working on its behalf. Therefore, it can not remain in a fixed or steady-state condition for too long a period of time. If it enters a tendency to decrease in size, it will tend to decrease itself to the final point of total elimination. Thus to maintain itself, it must indulge in a growth operation that must be continued on a prolonged basis. In other words, it is either grow or die.

Although there is a tendency for man-made organizations to grow, there is a limit to a final size. Nothing can be bigger than the elements available for its total use. A man-made group can not be larger than the total number of people available. In addition, nothing can be bigger than the maximum geometrical confines that are existing or that are available. Thus any particular man-made organization is limited to the final size to which it can grow.

But the rule is either grow or die. Even though it is limited, the organization will tend to continue its growth. This ten-

171

dency in the face of limitation, coupled with an ignorance of the affecting aspects of Logic and of Time Theory, will cause a number of special problems. To counter these, a number of Logic and pseudo-Logic type changes will be implemented. These will aggravate the problems further.

These problems will appear at first as rumblings. Things that always worked before, will not fit into the usual operations. Slowdown and breakdown will be manifested in the regular operations. New things will be tried and more effort will have to be expended just to implement what previously was simple and straightforward in the past. Thus more and more effort will produce less and less, but will have to be expended to keep from failing.

In an attempt to counter all these happenings in the final portion of its existence cycle, Logic will dictate that some form of partial self-destruction be imposed upon the ungainly large man-made organization. For a government in this condition, this necessitates and means war. From a Logical point of view, nothing else can or will work. In the outward appearances, most of the usual values will have to be set aside.

The deposing of important values will be very prominent in any man-made organization when it becomes too large. In this unwieldy condition, priorities must change. They will do this in a very Logical fashion. It will take place in a Logical sequential order involving an entire series of happenings. At the origination of the organization, usually some form of purpose or high ideal is stated. With one or more of these considered important reasons, the organization is formed and developed. These reasons take top priority in the organization, at least in the beginning. As time goes by, the "practical" demands of the organization become increasingly more important. If the organization should cease to exist, then the high ideals too must cease to exist. Therefore, the maintenance of the organization moves into top importance. Monies must be provided to pay bills, salaries, and upkeep. Administration must be provided and, with and for the higher level jobs, politics must enter the scene. Expansion, promotion, more people, buildings, and fund raising move to positions of ever higher importance. As these become more and more important, the guiding original ideals and purposes are relegated to lesser positions. Thus in the Logical sequence of happenings in the developing man-made organization, the priorities given the different values change so that original ideals and intents eventually become downgraded from their initial lofty heights.

As its emphasis on priorities changes, the man-made organization becomes more and more predictable in its man-induced operations. Emphasis is placed on the "practical" priorities. In Education, the needs shift from those of the students to those of the teachers. In Religion, the shift is away from the philosophies and ascetic values, and the priority is placed on the administrational aspects. The same will be true for government and all the other man-made organizations.

During the duration of its life cycle, almost all man-made organizations exhibit the same sets of characteristics. At the beginning, there are intent, purpose, and high ideals. As the organizations develop, these references give way to the "practical" needs for maintenance and growth. In the final phases, there is almost complete reversal of priorities. Extra efforts must be expended as the results slacken off. Values and meaning are pushed aside. More and more acceptance settles in. Tolerance of a wider range of things can be noted, even to tolerance of impropriety. Actions become more mechanical rather than being motivated by high type values. Emphasis centers on perpetuating the individual rather than the organization.

Thus existing organizations falter and become ripe for change, failure, or takeover. Logic and indeed all types of referencing will then fail no matter how well applied at this stage. Like the Universe itself, new aspects and side effects will occur and new systems and new organizations will tend to then come into being.

Part V

THEOLOGY AND SCIENCE

18

USING THEOLOGY TO SOLVE DIFFICULT PROBLEMS IN SCIENCE

"Hear instruction, and be wise, and refuse it not."

(The Bible, O.T., Proverbs 8:33)

If we are to learn anything from our attempts to determine knowledge, it is that rarely does an answer to a difficult problem come from just one source or just one field of learning. Rather such an answer must come from a group of fields, usually in some ordered relationship. Often it is the acquisition of only one key piece of necessary information that can trigger off the whole associated problem solving process. In numerous instances of complex situations, Theology can be used to provide and develop such necessary and often critical information to facilitate the solving of many difficult problems in science.

When most people consider the subject of Theology, they usually think of it only in terms of its very special capability, the referencing of religious subjects. However, Theology is much more inclusive than this and can be used for far more

177

than just this one possiblity. Indeed, it can be utilized to examine varied subject areas. These numerous subjects can all fit into the total encompassing format of Theology where each can be given extended and very special perspective.

It is said in Theology, that God is the reference of everything in the Universe. God is considered the source or fountainhead from which everything comes into being. From this, it would follow that all technology and science, as well as the entire Universe, must stem from God. Thus Theology Theory must also have the capability of directly referencing various aspects of science.

Science represents just one of the many subject areas that can be included for study under Theology. So far, we have been using various aspects of science to reference the Theological studies. To prove how unique and helpful Theology can really be, we now reverse this usual process and use aspects of Theology to reference and deal with difficult problems in Science.

To illustrate this extra capability of Theology, a number of unusual examples are being cited herein. The actual solution to each cited problem represents a composite effort involving various specific aspects associated with a number of different disciplines of knowledge. Yet each of these examples is illustrative of a problem situation wherein the solution was initiated by using Theological parameters. These examples include the following:

1. Mathematically deriving the Speed of Light.
2. Examination of the opto-biological process of eyesight with emphasis on the determination of the location of the final image produced as an end result of that process.
3. Development of the origin of each species to deter-

mine how the first or archetype of each category of life came about.

4. Evaluation and interpretation of personality and other characteristics of the human being, using the concept of the Soul.

5. Determination of the repeating Cyclical variations of the Universe.

6. Determination of the actual age and the size of the present existent Universe.

To provide for the desired derivation of Item #1, the particular initiating Theological parameter was the Bible number of "12." This number is repeated so many times in The Bible that its very emphasis signified something of significance. So important is this interpreting discussion that it is presented in detail separately in Chapter 19 herein.

For Item #2 concerning the location of the final image that is developed in the process involved with eyesight, the associated location was determined to be in the Fourth Group of the geometrical dimensional arrangements of the Universe. Thus the process of eyesight is considered a multidimensional operation with the initial observation made and referenced in the conventional Euclidean (or regular 3-dimensional) geometry which is called the "First Group." Then operations occur in the memory section of the Second Group. All this is under the control of the fixed memory located in the Third Group. (See the book of LIFE for a more detailed discussion of these included operations and dimensional groups.) Finally the end image is resolved and produced in the Fourth Group. This conclusion was obtained from an analysis that is also referenced by the Bible number "12." Further discussion of this formation of the final image of eyesight will also be found in Chapter 19.

179

To provide for the determination of the origin of each first type of Life-form (Item #3), a dual Theological referencing was used. The first clue concerning how to proceed came from the New Testament of the Holy Bible in the statement:

". . . God, the firstborn of every creature."

(Colosseans 1:15)

When this statement is taken literally, then the manifestation of God precedes any and all forms of Life. Therefore the representation of God should be used in any attempt of an origin of Life derivation. For a mathematical interpretation, this means that a mathematical value for God should be used in the included derivation. Of the four derivations of God (see Chapters 7, 8, 9, and 10 in Section II herein), Chapter 7 takes on the most direct bearing, since it is concerned with the concept of the Creation of God. This is especially important since we are dealing with the creation of a new form of Life. In addition, the approach of Chapter 7 also provides a mathematical value that results from the included Creation of God. When this value is utilized in the derivations of Life, the first mathematically meaningful results are obtained. This derivation and its discussion are presented in greater detail in the book of LIFE in the chapter entitled "Origin of Life and Species."

For the examination of personality and other operational characteristics of the human being (Item #4), the concept of the Soul becomes the overwhelming choice with which to begin such work. From the Theological point of view, the Soul is the reference of the human being. It provides the basis for all operations relating to the activities of the human existence. IT SETS UP THE CONDITIONS AND THE RAISON D'ETRE FOR ALL HUMAN QUALITIES AND

ASPECTS SUCH AS LIKES AND DISLIKES, TALENTS, PHOBIAS, ATTITUDES, ETC. So important is the concept of the Soul to Theology that it is developed and discussed separately in Chapter 11 herein. The mathematical and especially the geometrical interpretation of the Soul is further used to reference and develop a number of complex aspects of Life, which are also included in the book of LIFE.

To provide for the determination of the Repeating Cyclical Variations in the Universe (Item #5), a number of repeating qualities were noted in the Theological concepts of Creation and existence. No matter when, how, or why the Universe has its initiation for its Creation, it always proceeds in the same ordered sequence of steps. The first thing that is always created is and must be the phenomenon of God (see Chapter 6). A repeating specific order is the primary requirement for a cycle. The existent Universe meets this condition as well as a number of other aspects. Again, this topic is considered to be so important that it is presented in detail separately in Chapter 23.

Perhaps the most unusual of this group of examined subject items is the determination of the age and the size of the existent Universe (Item #6). For this determination, we begin by posing a set of questions which are led by a unique apparent coincidence that has occurred in Theology. This unique coincidence involves the situation in which the origins of most of the world's major Religions all formally began during the same approximate time period in history. From this very special aspect of Theology which we utilize to initiate the solution, we move on to other disciplines of knowledge to fully deal with the entire problem. This determination is presented in its entirety in Chapter 20.

THE APPLICATIONS AND USES OF THEOLOGY ARE ALMOST BEYOND LIMIT. Theology actually can be considered as including and covering all other subject areas.

It can often offer an explanation when other subject areas have reached an impasse. Even in the most complex problem situation, Theology can usually be counted upon to present at least some type of initiating explanation. For example, when the very difficult concept of the extensions of existence are considered with respect to Life, the associated development in Life Theory is so very complex that it appears almost insurmountable to handle. However, Theology Theory can introduce this topic on a direct basis by looking at this subject through the concept of the Soul.

The explanations using Theology Theory are usually simpler than many other types because they deal with subject material that is at once more familiar and definitely more understandable. People can relate more easily to a presentation in Theology than to one in advanced Physics. Thus Theology can be used to introduce almost any high level subject.

One of the most unusual aspects of Theology Theory is that it can be directly related to Time Theory. The basis of Theology Theory is God. It has been stated that the reference or Soul of God has been identified as being the same as the reference or noumenon of Time. Since the references of two separate concepts can be identified with each other, many aspects of one concept can be directly interchanged with similar aspects of the other. Thus the simpler explanations of Theology Theory can be used to begin almost any analysis. After these Theological beginnings are established, the unique science-type orientation of Time Theory can be used to provide further specific interpretation of the included problem.

The true capability and power of Theology is much greater than that which even the most ardent followers of Religion would have ever dared to realize. Theology represents so much more than just the philosophy of Religion. In this capacity, its intrinsic development has led it inexorably to a position of overall perspective, encompassing everything in the Universe. Within this huge framework, it is able to lead the way to understanding in numerous fields of knowledge. It can provide meaning and purpose when other systems of thought can not be applied. It truly becomes the effective intermediary between the Universe and Man.

19

DERIVATION OF THE SPEED OF LIGHT USING THE BIBLE NUMBER

"And God said, Let there be light: and there was light. And God saw the light, that it was good: and God divided the light from the darkness."

(The Bible, O.T., Genesis 1:3-4)

When anything is emphasized and is repeated again and again, it often represents an unusual symbolism that should be given special attention for additional interpretation. Such is the case with the number "12" which appears repeatedly in The Bible. The frequency with which this number appears suggests that some special significance is involved, and that it can be used for other than its immediate and initially intended purpose. Indeed, upon the examination of the developed Existence charts and tabulations, it was found that this number was included. When these circumstances were investigated further and in more detail, the results led to new concepts related to the operations associated with light energy. Of particular importance, mathematical interpretations resulted in new theoretical derivations of the speed of light!

The number "12" appears so many times in both the Old

184

and the New Testaments of The Bible that it could be considered as being a holy number. For examples, there are the 12 Tribes of Israel, the 12 Apostles of Jesus, the 12 Gates of Jerusalem, and the 12 Sons of Jacob. Especially, the last section of the Bible (Revelation) cites "12" in numerous verses. Twelve (12) can be further identified with various other things. There are the 12 signs of the Zodiac, the 12 months of the year, the 12 hours in a day, the 12 hours in the night, and the 12 persons on a jury. In mathematics, there is the duodecimal system (counting by twelves). In geometry, there is the dodecahedron which is a 3-dimensional figure consisting of 12 plane faces.

With "12" emphasized in such a pronounced way, it became mandatory to examine the various functions and concepts developed in all of the research performed herein, to find which of these included the number "12." This value was found in the relationship involving the ordered set of the Steps of Existence developed in the book of EXISTENCE.

In this ordered or sequentially arranged Steps of Existence, the number "12" appears in the Fourth Step. Each of the steps of this series function, represents the order in which the significant changes occur in the development of the existent Universe after Creation. In mathematics, each of these steps can be considered as a "Step Function" in which a perceptible distinct change takes place.

Within the mathematical boundaries associated with each step, there is a set of "points." These represent the included tasks or operations of the Universe that must be completed before we can move on to the next step. With each step of development after Creation, there is relatively much more in the Universe than there was before that step. Actually the completion of each step results in a doubling of the previously developed contents of the Universe. With more things in the Universe, there is more to deal with and more to do before we can move on to the next step. Therefore, as the identification or order number of the steps (S) increases, the number of the included points (P) also increases, but at the much faster rate as shown by the relationship:

$$P = 3 \times (2)^{S-2}$$

It will be seen that, for the Fourth Step after Creation, "S" is equal to 4. Accordingly, "P" is equal to 12.

The Fourth Step has two special mathematical aspects whose significance should also be noted here. The notation of the "Steps" can further be applied to the geometrical inference of dimensional concepts. Thus the Fourth Step can also represent the Fourth Dimension. Among other considerations, the Fourth Dimension holds a unique geometrical position since previous series-type situations will repeat themselves after the Fourth Dimension is reached. The fact that the 12 points (Bible Number) occur in the Fourth Step indicates mathematically that division by 4 (repeating aspect) and the fourth root (dimensional aspect) are both involved.

From the operations point of view of the Universe, it is the P-number "12" which becomes the base value (of the functional notation). The Step-number "4" is such that it can be applied in a manner to mathematically operate upon the base (12). Since at the Fourth Step after Creation, the highest available single quantity is "12," then any mathematical operation performed upon this number must result in a lower value, because this maximum quantity can not be exceeded at this time.

Accordingly, of the six basic mathematical operations of

1. Addition
2. Subtraction
3. Multiplication

4. Division
5. Powers
6. Roots

only Subtraction, Division, and Roots will produce results which are less than the original base number on which they operate. Using these latter operations, we can tabulate the associated results on the chart shown in Figure 3.

The results of these tabulated operations show the three new numerical bases of 8, 3, and 1.86 as the developed values. The first of these is an octal base which has significance in the development and the interpretation of the E-L-M Tabulations of Existence Theory.

BASE	OPERATION	OPERATOR	RESULT
12	Minus	4	8
12	Divided	4	3
12	to the Root of	4	1.86

FIGURE 3 - MATHEMATICAL OPERATIONS
UPON THE BASE "12"

However, it is the "Division by 4" and the "Fourth Root" that are of the most importance to the present discussion. It will be seen that the results of these two functions provide the basic numerical values (except for the exponents) of the conventional figure of the speed of light as expressed in the Metric system (3) and in the English system (1.86).

The formula presented for the determination of the number of points (P) for each particular step (S), used an adjustment of "2" on the "S" value. In the shown chart, the first mathematical operation is a subtraction function. If this subtraction is continued again using the adjustment value of "2" but this time taken from the reference value of "12," the result is 10. This quantity of "10" is also the sum total of all the previous numbers of points associated with Steps 1, 2, and 3 ($1 + 3 + 6$ respectively). Just as "12" was a base, the number "10" now developed is considered and used as a base. The result using the extra quantity of "10" is the exponentiation which produces 10^{10}. This is now applied to the next number (3) which was developed on the previous chart, and we obtain

$$3 \times 10^{10}$$

which is the Metric value of the speed of light expressed in centimeters per second.

It was noted that the second step on the chart involved the mathematical function or process of division. The adjustment value of "2" is still in effect and is used again. Since the process of division has been cited, the previously acquired value of "10" is now divided by 2. When this result is applied to the value previously obtained and shown in the third step on the chart, we obtain

$$1.86 \times 10^5$$

188

which can be compared favorably to the English value for the speed of light expressed in miles per second. Coupling these Metric and English units with their respective numerical values, we obtain

$$3.00 \times 10^{10} \text{ cm/sec}$$
$$1.86 \times 10^{5} \text{ miles/sec}$$

Thus the Bible number of "12" has indicated the use of the function of twelve, or f(12), which provides the basis for a simultaneous derivation of the conventional speed of light in terms of both the Metric and the English units.

All of the foregoing information in this chapter has been used to deal with theoretical aspects of light energy. These have been developed from interpretations from the concept of the "Steps of Existence." Specifically due to the Bible number "12," we have been led to the Fourth of these steps. Now let us examine some of the other implications of this identification.

One of the important questions of Science is — When does light energy first appear after the event of the Creation of the Universe? It has already been stated that the first identification of light energy is with the Fourth Step of Existence. These Steps of Existence have been mathematically derived to show the sequential order of the way that the Universe developed after its initial Creation. Each of these Steps represents a set of associated operations and happenings (also called out as "points") that take place or are involved in the Universal development. With the identification of light energy with the fourth of these steps, it can be concluded that that which is called light first appears in the Fourth Step after Creation. Thus the development of light is not immediate, but rather takes several intermediate or other steps from its inception prior to the time when it actually appears.

The Holy Bible concurs that light was not immediately available at the Creation of the Universe. The first mention of light is in the *third* verse, which states

And God said, Let there be light: and there was light.

(Genesis 1:3)

Other things were listed as happening or coming before light.

1. In the beginning God created the heaven and the earth.
2. And the earth was without form, and void; and darkness was upon the face of the deep. And the Spirit of God moved upon the face of the waters.

(Genesis 1:1-2)

Thus darkness (or the lack of light) is specifically called out as a distinct condition at the Creation. In addition, God is the first thing cited. Indeed, it has already been shown (see Chapter 6) that the phenomenon of God was the first thing created in the Universe. Thus Step 1 of the Steps of Existence is identified as being totally and only concerned with the creation of the phenomenon of God in the existent Universe.

After God, the next things mentioned include heaven, the earth, the waters, and the Spirit of God. Since Steps 1 and 4 have already been accounted for, it would appear that these things just mentioned could be associated with Steps 2 and 3.

Within this chapter, we have been considering aspects of operations and happenings associated with light and energy. There is another interpretation of the Fourth Step of Existence which can be applied to the concept of eyesight. The end portion of the process of eyesight is the resulting final image that is produced "internally" within the subject form of life that is doing the viewing. However, although this final image is considered internal, the question is exactly where is this image actually produced? Investigation of this question (see the book of LIFE) has indicated that this final image of eyesight is produced outside the 3-dimensional confines of the physical presence so that it would be in another dimensional group. If the regular 3-dimensional boundaries are considered to be called the First Dimensional Group, then the Fourth Step of Existence would imply the Fourth Dimensional Group. Since light has already been associated with this Fourth Step, then the process of eyesight (which is considered to be a multi-dimensional activity) will have its culmination in the Fourth Dimensional Group of the existent Universe (see Figure 2).

Thus from the Bible number of "12," the function of twelve, or f(12), has produced various instances of operations involving light energy.

As an epilogue to this chapter, there is a most unusual additional aspect that must be noted due to the inclusion of the introductory selection from Scriptures which was added to the beginning of the chapter after it was written. This selection reads:

"And God *SAW* the light" (The Bible, O.T., Genesis 1:4).

It is especially fitting that this selection from Scriptures be used to introduce this chapter. This selection marks the first time in The Bible that the word "saw" appears. This word refers to the process of seeing or eyesight. The occurrence of the final portion of this process (where the final image is actually formed) has just been disclosed in this chapter as taking place in the *FOURTH* Group of geometrical dimensions of the Universe. It is interesting to note that the word "saw" appears for the first time in the FOURTH verse of The Bible.

20

THEOLOGICAL DETERMINATION OF THE AGE AND SIZE OF THE UNIVERSE

"Have ye not known? have ye not heard? hath it not been told you from the beginning? have ye not understood from the foundations of the earth?"

(The Bible, O.T., Isaiah 40:21)

As the prelude for establishing many of the Theological concepts, numerous scientific references have first been applied. Now we are reversing this usual procedure to demonstrate the special capability of Theology Theory to directly reference aspects of Science.

This Theological capability shall be demonstrated by examining the very difficult question concerning the determination of the present age of the Universe. This represents a composite task which involves a number of different fields of knowledge. Leading into this task is a special particular grouping of a set of some of the most important events that have ever happened in Theology. The inference of this collective set of events bears upon an unusual relationship in Time Theory. From here, we move to comparative aspects in Existence Theory which provide for the overall interpretation. The final details and conclusions are obtained by bringing in and using specific aspects of Physics, Astronomy, Geology, and Mathematics.

This determination was made possible through the realization of the remarkable coincidence that took place when a number of highly important separate Theological happenings all occurred at approximately the same period in history. The fact that all of these happenings coincided within the same relative time period, implies that there was a particular Theological reason associated with all of these events. It is toward this particular inference that we will now direct our attention.

Let us begin with an important observation concerning Christianity. Approximately 2,000 years ago, the central figure of Christianity, Jesus Christ, was born in the Middle East and lived through that very special Life-time from which developed that major Religion which bears His name. Since everything in Theology has a reason, why was this particular time, the time of Jesus? Concerning this particular time, why was it not 10,000 years earlier or perhaps 2,000 years later? In other words, why was this the time that was Theologically chosen for the occurrence of the Life of Jesus?

Approximately 2,500 years ago another great person, Gautama Buddha, (from whom Buddhism had its origins) went through the very special occurrence of His Life-time in India. Again it may be asked — Why did this occur at this particular time? Why not some other time?

Approximately 2,500 years ago, the two great men of China, Lao-tse and Kung-Fu-tse (Confucius), went through the occurrence of their life-times. Again, why did these occur at this particular time? Why not some other time?

Approximately 2,400 years ago, the great philosophers of Greece, including Plato and Aristotle, went through the occurrence of their lives. Again, why did this occur at this particular time?

Approximately 2,600 years ago, the great Persian Zoroaster (or Zarathustra), founder of Zoroastrianism, went through the occurrence of His Life. Again, why did this occur at this particular time?

Approximately 2,500 years ago in the Middle East, it is estimated that the first major portions of the Old Testament were collected together and written down in this initial organization of the Judaic Bible. Again, why at this time?

Approximately 2,500 years ago Jainism, a Religion with certain similar aspects to Hinduism and Buddhism, was founded in India. Again, why this event at this time?

Approximately 2,600 years ago Shintoism, the first major Religion of Japan, is believed to have originated. Again, why did this event occur at this time?

Thus within the same approximate time period, we find significant events touching upon Hinduism and also taking place in Judaism, Zoroastrianism, Buddhism, Christianity, Confucianism, Shintoism, Jainism, and the Golden Age of Greece. All of these occurrences represent happenings of the very highest intellectual nature. All of these represent definitely advanced achievements of the human thinking process. As such, all of these citations represent wisdom in every sense of this concept.

The wisdom involved in all these cited examples ranks among the very highest of all mankind's intellecutal achievements. Indeed in pure philosophy, the collective works of the Greek philosophers (Socrates, Plato, Aristotle, etc) during the Golden Age of Greece is unmatched in the overall scope of its total content. So complete was the totality of the philosophical questions posed, that even today after some 2,500 years, almost no really new questions have been set forth.

Especially for Theology, this period was truly a time of achievement. There was the outright creation of Christianity, Buddhism, Zoroastrianism, Jainism, Shintoism, and Confucianism. There were important developments in Judaism and

Hinduism. The seeds of Islam were being planted and were soon to bear fruit. Thus there were major happenings occurring in all of the world's great Religions. The height of these Theological achievements during this time is truly unequaled in all of recorded history, neither before nor since this period.

The present twentieth century has been an outstanding one for scientific progress and technology. The quality and extent of the technical developments are truly remarkable. Yet in the greater perspective of comparative evaluation, the cited Golden Time of Theology exceeds even these technological developments. Although it has been said before, the importance of the following postulate remains unalterable. The requirements for the Soul take precedence over those for the body.

Thus it is that the period of approximately 2,000 to 2,500 years ago represents a special time of unparalleled intellectual achievement in the recorded history of Mankind. It is truly the period of the greatest wisdom of all time.

The fact that a time period is involved and the fact that this time period is one of great wisdom, are both of especial importance in Time Theory. Here these happenings and events can be further described in terms of a time-sequence representation which can be expressed and expanded into a mathematical infinite-series function. In its infinite-series form, such a function is difficult to examine and handle. However, there are certain aspects of such a function which are independent of the actual mathematics and define particular geometric points or ratios which must occur at specific locations along the function. It has been separately established (see the books of TIME and EXISTENCE) that a complete time sequence involving almost any operation, happening, or entity will have five special points associated with it that will take priority regardless of the included mathematics of the subject function. These five special points and their associated ratio locations along the mathematical series function are listed as follows:

Point	Position
1. Initiation	0
2. Sex Point	1/8
3. Wisdom Point	1/2
4. Phase-Out Point	7/8
5. Termination	1

With respect to these points, the first or Initiation Point occurs right at the beginning of the mathematical series function so its location position is at the start or zero (0). The last or Termination Point occurs at the very end or the 100% completion location which is one (1) on the relative position scale. The other points occur at intermediate positions along the series function in accordance with their listed proportion. The names of all these various points reflect either their operational aspect or the area of specific research in which they were originally developed.

It is the third point on the list which is of special interest to our immediate discussions. This third or Wisdom Point was determined as a result of research into the time relationships involving the functioning of the human thinking process. It was found that at the exact mid-point of the associated mathematical time-series function, the conditions necessary for that situation which is called "wisdom" become available to support highly advanced thinking. When these conditions do become available, an indication that this has happened can be found as a manifestation of a grouping of profound wisdom which was not present before this time. When and if this manifestation does occur for the first time (for it need not occur at all), it will do so at the exact half-way point of the included series time function.

It is the intent of our examinations, to determine the present age of the existent Universe. Since age is associated with time concepts, it can be expressed in terms of a series time-function. One of the characteristics of such a series time function is that there is a set of special points that can identify how far along the series function the associated time operations have progressed. The specific aspects identified with each point are exact and unalterable and even take priority over the included mathematics of the function itself. In applying the concept of these special points, the objective is to examine the included characteristics of the manifested situation under study to see if it compares favorably with that of one of the special points. One of these is the Wisdom Point, whose importance lies in its capability to designate when the subject has reached the mid-way point in its operations.

Presentations in this chapter have shown that there was a very special grouping in a relatively short time period of Theological instances involving the most profound wisdom that the world has ever known. This has been identified as collectively happening in that period of history dating back 2,000 to 2,500 years ago. Since this particular collection of Theological wisdom is so outstanding, it is considered to be a manifestation that can be compared very favorably with the special Wisdom Point. This particular Wisdom Point, due to definition and development, is identified and associated with the existent Universe, as an indication that it has arrived at the middle of its time span. THEREFORE, THE AGE OF THE EXISTENT UNIVERSE IS CONSIDERED TO HAVE REACHED THE HALF-WAY POINT IN ITS FULL OPERATIONAL TIME CYCLE AT A TIME AP-PROXIMATELY 2,000 YEARS AGO.

With the acquisition of this one-half value, we now have one of the most difficult parts of our determination. To obtain this age in terms of the actual number of years, the next step requires the applied use of other disciplines of knowledge. Since the "year" is a man-made or assigned term, the use of the scientific concepts of Existence and Time will be invoked, along with selected aspects of Physics, Astronomy, Geology, and Mathematics to provide for the necessary development.

With respect to its included operations, there is a distinct relationship involving the Existence of the Universe with comparison to Time. This relationship can be developed in mathematics and geometry. In graphical form it is called the "Generalized Curve of Existence" and is shown in Figure 4. It was established in the book of EXISTENCE using a number of Physics and Mathematical derivations. It shows the generalized cycle of existence which is applicable to all operations, happenings, and entities — including the Universe itself.

In its overall interpretation, the Generalized Curve of Existence shows the specific times of Creation, initial development, point of maximum development, decline, and finally Termination. The relative time values are presented along the abscissa in a horizontal time base scale that is developed in Time Theory. For the Universe, this becomes an octal scale which goes linearly from zero (Initiation) to the value of one (Termination).

This Generalized Curve can be used to describe the development of the existent Universe, or any existence (including human life), in accordance with the following: (Note — the associated time period ratios are shown in parenthesis)

1. The event of Creation (0).
2. Universe expanding at an increasing accelerating rate (0 to 1/8).
3. Universe expanding at maximum accelerating rate (1/8).
4. Universe expanding at a decreasing accelerating rate (1/8 to 1/3).

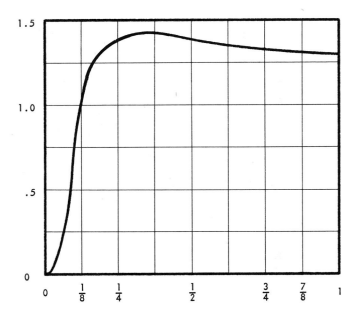

Relative Existence

Proportion of Existence Cycle
(or Time Cycle)

FIGURE 4 — GENERALIZED CURVE OF EXISTENCE

199

5. Universe at zero accelerating rate of expansion, approximate point of linear displacement (1/3).
6. Universe in condition of decline, or expanding at a negative accelerating rate (1/3 to 1).
7. The event of Termination (1).

From the Curve and the itemized list of included information, the point of the maximum development of existence is at approximately 1/3 of the Time-scale abscissa. With respect to the existent Universe, this represents the situation where the accelerating rate of expansion is zero. For this condition, optical observations using Astronomy telescope techniques should show that there was neither accelerating expansion nor contraction. Therefore, any visible extremely-far celestial objects should be seen to be moving away from the Earth at linearly increasing speeds that are related to each other in direct proportion to the extent of the distances involved. This would mean that observation of the light spectra of distant galaxies should show uniform displacement effects in these spectral patterns that were approximately linear and directly proportional to the ratio of the included distances.

This is the approximate situation that is being observed at Astronomical Observatories at various parts of the world at the present time. This is actually the situation that should be in effect at the 1/3 time-cycle point. YET, FROM THE THEOLOGICAL ANALYSIS INVOLVING THE CONCEPT OF THE WISDOM POINT, IT IS INDICATED THAT THE UNIVERSE IS APPROXIMATELY NOW AT THE 1/2 TIME-CYCLE POINT. The resulting difference is considered to be due to the vast distances involved and the fact that it takes light a huge amount of finite time to traverse such great distances. Even though the speed of light is very fast, when it has to travel through huge distances it will require a proportionally large amount of time. If we could determine a time value for the relative time-scale that is represented to be between the 1/3 and the 1/2 time cycle points on the Generalized Curve of Existence (as it is applied to the Universe), we would then have the missing piece of information that is necessary to calculate both the present age of the Universe and a good estimation of its physical size.

The key to all this, is to establish another fact concerning the 1/3 time-cycle point. Of the possible considerations, this fact should be something of importance since it is associated with the Earth. For the Earth has a time-history all its own, and yet will also follow the prescribed sequences noted by the Generalized Curve of Existence.

Consider again the Theological happenings that were cited to be in association with the Wisdom Point and examine WHERE all these events took place. Although the interpretation was for the Universe, the location of all these happenings was the Earth. In Time Theory, it can be shown that, for a coincidence of happenings involving different entities, any interpretation developed for any one of these entities can be applied to all. The Theological happenings of 2,000 to 2,500 years ago have indicated that the Universe had reached the Wisdom Point or the half-way mark in its age at that time. Since these events took place on the Earth, then the Earth too is considered to have reached the mid-point of its age coincidentally at that time period as well.

Although the mid-points of the ages of the Earth and the Universe coincide, the Earth is considered to be much younger than the Universe. Indeed, Astronomy evaluations have indicated that the Earth is younger than the Sun and that the Sun, in turn, is younger than many other stars. The question that comes to mind now is — Where on the Generalized Curve of Existence can we identify the origination of the Earth?

The 1/3 time-cycle point, which is the approximate point of maximum development in the Universe, is also considered to be the location in time of the creation of the Earth. This point marks the end of the initial development period of the Universe which would culminate in Astronomical structural bodies that could support advanced Life-forms. Such celestial bodies originated in time at approximately the 1/3 time-cycle point, would tend to be more in the steady-state physical and geometrical considerations since the conditions of the Universe had stabilized. These celestial bodies would be of a fixed size that was neither too large (so as to avoid too strong a gravity field) nor too small (so it could still retain air in its surrounding atmosphere). These bodies would also require the abundance of a large amount of stable solid material in their make-up mix. In addition, as called out in numerous Religious Scriptures, large amounts of water in liquid form would also be required. The liquid requirement would necessitate that the associated temperatures be confined within certain fixed narrow ranges. These basic conditions could only be obtained at or after the 1/3 time cycle point. Some of these requirements (like Temperature) could only be made available if the celestial body was in a suitable Astronomical structure (like an orbit) in proximity to a star. The occurrence of such a structure is more probable in the development period of the Universe either at or before the 1/3 time-cycle point. Therefore, taking all these requirements into account, the result would be that a celestial body like the Earth would have been originated at the 1/3 time-cycle point as depicted on the Generalized Curve of Existence. Thus the age of the Earth is considered to be counted from its creation at the 1/3 time-cycle point to the present 1/2 time-cycle point.

Geological interpretation of the age of the Earth has placed it at approximately 4 billion years old. This figure may vary somewhat depending upon the tests, such as the use of a variety of methods involving radioactivity, and the included specified initial conditions. However, this 4 billion year value is believed to be a reasonably good estimation of the age of the Earth and accordingly will be used for this important calibration of time. (Should this value be improved upon in the future, then the new verified figure could be substituted at this point in the age determination). Thus for calibration purposes, the length of time involved from the creation of the Earth (at the 1/3 time-cycle point) to the present (or 1/2 time-cycle point) is considered to be 4 billion years.

This 4 billion years represents 1/3 of the total time in years that are involved from the actual Creation of the Universe (0 time-cycle point) to the 1/2 time-cycle point of the included overall existence cycle of the Universe. This amount of 1/3 is obtained as follows:

The time scale value between the 1/2 and the 1/3 time-cycle points is:

$$1/2 - 1/3 = 3/6 - 2/6 = 1/6 \text{ which is } 1/3 \text{ of } 3/6$$

Thus the age of the existent Universe to the present is 4 billion years times 3, or approximately a total of
12 BILLION YEARS.

The present age of the Universe is stated to be 12 billion years. Actually this would have been the age during the period of 2,000 to 2,500 years ago. However, it should be noted that a few thousand years one way or the other will not really affect our interpretations due to the huge total time periods that are actually involved.

With this present age established, some additional conclusions are now possible. This age is applicable to the half-way point of the total existence. Therefore, the total time cycle of the entire existent Universe is anticipated to be 24 billion years from the moment of Creation to the final Termination (provided that there is no catastrophic premature Termination before this estimated time of final maturity).

Since the Earth is considered to be 4 billion years old at the present time, it is anticipated that its total cycle of existence will last 8 billion years. Again this estimation is based on the provision that there will be no catastrophic premature termination before this time of final maturity.

With the establishment of these listed ages, full calibration has been provided (in terms of years) for the time-base abscissa on the Generalized Curve of Existence for the existent Universe. Thus, as required, other data can be extrapolated from this reference curve.

An estimation of the SIZE of the Universe can be made using the information developed in this chapter. It has been previously mentioned that the Astronomers are observing the Universe as appearing as though it has reached the 1/3 time-cycle point. These sightings are being made at present, and actually represents the 1/2 time-cycle point. The cause of this delay is due to the actual time it takes light to traverse these huge included distances. The time difference between the 1/3 and the 1/2 time-cycle points on the General Curve of Existence has been already estimated to be 4 billion years. Since light travelling at the conventional speed of light covers a distance of approximately 6 trillion miles in one year, the total distance involved due to the time delay difference is:

$$\text{4 billion years x 6 trillion miles/year} =$$
$$\textit{24 billion trillion miles}$$

This figure, which can also be expressed as 24×10^{21} miles represents the SHORTEST possible length from the Earth to the end of the physical (or conventional Euclidean or 3-dimensional) Universe. Since the Earth originated well after the Creation of the Universe, it (the Earth) certainly can not be anywhere near its (the Universe) center. Thus the expressed figure represents just one possible radial length which is subject to change depending upon future sightings and associated distance estimations.

The maximum possible distance from the Earth to an end of the Universe can be derived by projecting a line from the Earth toward the center of the Universe. Then this line would be continued through and past this center until its extension reaches the far extremity of the Universe. Since we are dealing with the maximum possible distance, the Earth could be 8 billion light-years from this center. With the age of the Universe estimated at about 12 billion years, the second part of the extension line would be 12 billion light-years as the radius going from the center outward. The summation of both these maximum estimated distances, yields a total of $8 + 12 = 20$ billion light-years for the maximum possible distance at this time from the Earth to an end of the Euclidian portion of the Universe.

Thus the Universe is seen to be essentially a sphere with a radius of 12 billion light-years at the present time. Since the Earth is at least 4 billion light-years from the outer extremities, it must be located somewhere within an inner sphere concentric with the center of the Universe, and having a radius no larger than 8 billion light years. It is estimated that the Universe will continue to expand until it reaches the 7/8 portion of its existence cycle when its radius will have the maximum value of 21 billion light years. Then the existence operations will reverse as the Universe moves into its final or Termination Phase.

Part VI

TERMINATION

21

ASPECTS OF ESCHATOLOGY
(the End of the Universe)

"And judgment is turned away backward,"
(The Bible, O.T., Isaiah 59:14)

Eschatology is that branch of Theology that is concerned with the concept of last things. It deals with the operations, situations, and happenings that occur as a result of the ending of the Universe. It evaluates the causes and the consequences of these last happenings and attempts to place them in Theological perspective. Thus Eschatology deals with the final matters of Theology.

The aspects of Eschatology can be expanded to provide coverage of the more finite aspects of Theology. Since every person and every identifiable thing can be considered as a separate Universe in itself, Eschatology can also be applied to each person and each entity. Thus concepts such as death, destruction, resurrection, judgment of the Souls, entrance into heaven or hell, and freedom from the wheel of Samsara become applicable subjects under Eschatology.

According to Existence Theory, there is an end to everything that ever was, is, or ever will be. Indeed, where there is a beginning, there must eventually be an end. Thus for anything that is said to exist, there is a particular finite time limit for its existence. As this limit is approached, the cycle of the included existence comes to a close. After this end limit, the included existence is terminated, thereby completing and ending its particular time-cyclical pattern.

As an existent entity, the Universe also exhibits these time-cyclical variations. Its cycle begins at the Moment of Creation. Its development accelerates until it reaches a peak. Then its operations start to slow down and it goes into a general decline. Finally it moves into the total situation of Termination, after which, it ceases to be. This "Concept of the Repeating Cyclical Universe" is discussed in more detail in Chapter 23 herein.

The ending of the Universe is accompanied by a number of various specific happenings. Most important of these involves the operations that take place through the container or the geometry of existence. By virtue of Displacement Theory (see the book of PHYSICS), there is a geometry of existence which is built-up by displacement activities through all the dimensions. This displacement proceeds by the functioning of Time and Change. With each time-initiated increment of change, additional build-up occurs in the entity and its associated extensions of existence that are included throughout the various dimensions. This continues to operate reaching a peak and then declining in accordance to its identification with the associated mathematical series functions of existence. As long as this situation remains dynamic (i.e., so that there is continuance of change), the entity and its geometry will be maintained. However, when all this change activity comes to a halt and total staticism goes into effect, the associated entity is said to be terminated and therefore must cease to be.

For the most part, we will be considering the Termination of the Universe as occurring at the end of its full natural existence cycle. However, we need not be held to this particular situation. Depending upon the attendant conditions, catastrophic Termination of the Universe could conceivably occur at any time after Creation. Once it is initiated, the general sequence of events will be the same regardless of how the Termination was set into effect.

To provide the basis for our examination of Eschatology, the aspects of Termination must be in effect and the Universe will be considered as being in its final phase. The major aspects of the Termination that will be used to reference Eschatology, involve the following:

1. Termination of all happenings, functionings, and entities.
2. Cessation of Change.
3. Reversion from the Dynamic to the Static State.
4. Ending and reversal of geometry.
5. Elimination of wisdom, and then all thinking.
6. Ending of Life and all extensions of Life.

From these listed items, a number of inferences and conclusions can be discerned which are related to the Eschatology. Since everything is being affected by the Termination (Item 1), all change (Item 2) is ceasing at an ever accelerating rate. This seriously impedes the Universe in its maintaining of its existence since this process depends upon the functioning of change. Existence represents something that is dynamic. As this dynamic characteristic of change slows down and finally stops, that which is called existence must also stop. Thus the existent Universe finally ends by reverting (Item 3) to the static condition of the unchanging steady-state situation in which the Universe must Terminate.

With all these Termination happenings going into effect, a

particular one takes on special significance. This involves the geometry of the existent Universe. For as the Universe is ending, so must its included geometry of dimensions also come to an end (Item 4). Since this geometry of dimensions represents the container of the Universe, the cessation of the container means the inability to hold any contents. Thus the ending of the container becomes the very definite prelude to the absolute Termination of all existence.

During the Termination of the geometry of dimensions, some very important effects occur which bear directly upon the included Theology. First the outermost dimensions (those that were created last) are ended. Then this cessation process continues in the exact reverse order of the original build-up. Everything is reversing in the various geometric positions so that the thing last in (LI), becomes the first out (FO), which can be symbolically noted as LIFO. Contrasting this, the thing first in (FI) will be last out (LO) or FILO. This means that the existence of God which was the first creation in the Universe, will be the last thing remaining before the final Termination of all existence.

Thus the first thing in the beginning shall be the last thing in the end. The specific preciseness of this situation with respect to God is called out in The Bible which states:

"I am Alpha and Omega, the beginning and the end, the first and the last."

(Revelation 22:13)

In the overall Termination process, the various operations are taking place in definite stages in which the aspects of the included geometry play a very significant role. The existence of the dimensions is the primary requirement for the development of the thinking process which, in its ultimate organized form, provides for wisdom. In the reversing order of

Termination, wisdom is affected by first being degraded until its intrinsic capability is ended (Item 5). As these degradation effects continue, the capacity for thinking is lessened until it too is terminated.

As the total number of dimensions continues to decrease, the propensity of the Universe to allow and sustain the more complex Life-forms correspondingly decreases (Item 6). Since only the complex Life-forms are capable of providing the functions associated with advanced wisdom, the elimination of these higher order Life-forms correlates with the negation of wisdom.

The continuing Termination process causes a degrading action to take place at all the functional levels of the Universe. The degradation, occurring at the outer dimensional groups, affects the associated extensions of all types and forms of existence. As these extensions are stripped away, the basic existences must change to accommodate their lessening extensions.

The most significant portion of each existence is usually located in its outermost (or last) dimensional group. When this outermost dimensional group is terminated first, the physical portion of the particular subject existence ceases to be. The rest of the composite existence will still be there (in the Universe), at least until the remaining outer portions are stripped away in turn.

This concept of the stripping away of the outer dimensions one-at-a-time is particularly important to aspects of Life, especially to the relationship of Man with respect to Eschatology. It was mentioned that the last or outer dimensional group, in which Man exists, is terminated first. This geometrical group contains the physical presence, which is the most important (at least in terms of size) aspect that relates to Mankind. The Termination of this particular dimensional group will eliminate the physical presences of all the individuals of Mankind. With these physical presences gone, there will still remain (at least temporarily) all the extensions of existence that were associated with each individual life.

The most important of all the extensions of existence of Man is in the next inner dimensional group (after the physical presence), and represents that which is known as the Soul. As one portion of Eschatology implies, when the body or physical presence of Man is gone, then we must deal with the Soul.

At this stage in the Termination of the Universe, the geometry of the conventional (or Euclidean) dimensional group has just been eliminated. This elimination included the bodies (or physical presences) of all Life. With this major (sizewise) portion of the Life existence gone, the remaining aspect is the Soul. Since at this stage the Souls are no longer tied to their former body portions in what was described as a closed Life system (body and Soul both operational), the Soul is now independent in its functioning. As a free or unbound agent, the Soul now becomes a Spirit.

The Spirit is the storehouse of Life wherein there is an accumulation of every experience in which it participated in the past. Previous to becoming a Spirit, it was the Soul of another Life that manifested itself as an extension of existence in the next dimensional group. Here it was associated with the memory portion of the thinking process of the included Life-form. Due to the implications of this association, it acquired the composite characteristics of the other Life, including personality and stored past experiences. These past experiences were accumulated over the period of the subject Life's most recent existence (and that was closely associated with a particular body or physical presence). In addition, other past experiences were acquired from imprints imposed at the Moment of Conception which represented portions of memory data of previous other existences (see the book of

214

LIFE). Within this context, each Soul represents an accumulation of stored memory data of experiences traceable back along some path to the Origin of Life in the Universe. It includes at least some portion (however small) of every life that had some previous existence along this lineage path (or paths) back to the phenomenon of God, the first Life in the existent Universe.

With the roll-back of the dimensions to the geometrical group containing the unbound Souls, these Spirits (as they are now called) stand emphasized in their brief moment of dominant existence. Thus as the Theologies of most of the great religions have predicted, this becomes the special time associated with the Termination of the Universe when all the Souls (or more properly Spirits) of all the lives that ever were, now stand out in prominent emphasis.

The concept of "JUDGMENT" has often been invoked to describe what happens at this particular phase of the Termination. However, the concept of Judgment is NOT really applicable during Termination. This is because the process of Termination is a REVERSE situation. Everything is reverting or reversing back toward the origin. Judgment is a concept that can only happen in the forward (and not the reverse) direction of the standard activities of the Universe. As stated in the concept of Karma of Hinduism, judgment of past deeds is a direct consequence that is imprinted upon a next Life. As such, there can be no reverse judgment. Judgment can not be metered out to what went before. *Post hoc ergo propter hoc.* This quotation is sometimes argumentative, but certainly the reverse of this statement is never true.

As the Termination process continues, the roll-back of the dimensions will eliminate the dimensional group that contained the unbound Souls (or Spirits). With the elimination of this group and the next one as well, there will be a loss of all memory functions of all Life-forms. Thus all retained

215

knowledge of past experience relating to the most recent operational existence cycle of the Universe that is now ending will accordingly be lost.

With the termination of all memory capability, most of the functioning of the thinking processes will be ended. With Life and thinking being negated, the remaining aspects of Matter and Energy will move into the final operations of Termination. These processes will be eliminating each of the dimensional groups in turn and in reverse order in which they were created. With its container being eliminated, the Universe itself will come to an end.

The last thing in the Universe before final Termination will be the physical manifestation or the phenomenon of God. As the final act of Termination, this too will end, ending all existence and leaving just the Realm of Nothing as the only repository for the identification of God.

This area of Eschatology represents the only instance herein where there is a major divergence between discussions in this book and those in Religious Scriptures. In most of the subjects of the previous chapters of this book, there has been remarkable agreement with many of the statements and teachings of most of the major Theology that is presented in the various Scriptures of the world's seven most prominent Religions (Judaism, Christianity, Islam, Hinduism, Buddhism, Confucianism and Taoism, and Zoroastrianism). This agreement with Scriptures has held for all those instances where Man has been capable of witnessing either directly or indirectly (through research and other organized analyses) those portions of history dealt with by the Scriptures. It should be noted that divergence with Scriptures appears after that point in the Eschatology where Man is deprived of his sensory (vision, etc.) and his thinking capabilities.

Knowledge of recorded history has been obtained by being directly witnessed by Mankind. The results of this witnessing have been written down and recorded to form the various Scriptures such as the Judaic portion (the Old Testament) of the Holy Bible. Thus most of the major events of history have been directly observed and thereby made known to Man.

Even prehistoric times have been investigated by Man. A number of these associated happenings have been indirectly determined by composite means using different areas of knowledge. Through this continual probing involving considerable research and analysis, much has been learned by Man and recorded for posterity. Thus during his stay on Earth, Man has been the observer and researcher and has gained knowledge of many things relating to his past and present.

But with all his capabilities, Man can not directly observe and record the future. Man can not really know that which has not yet come to be. Thus Man is limited to knowledge involving the history or chronology of existence. Man can not use his senses to observe what does not exist.

Eschatology involves the ending of existence. With this ending, there is also an ending of Man's capability to observe any of the final results of Eschatology. Although Man can observe and hope to know, either directly or indirectly, the various happenings occurring from the Creation of the Universe to the beginning portion of Eschatology, he can never have any direct knowledge of Termination. Therefore, any such unreferenced attempts at interpretations, as may be presented in various Scriptures, will be prone to numerous errors. This becomes the major reason for any possible divergence of the concepts of Eschatology presented herein that may differ from those in Scriptures.

Thus the period of Eschatology involves the last phase of the existent Universe where total Termination occurs as the final result. Termination ends all existence including all aspects of God, Life, the Earth, Heaven, hell, and all other associated dwelling places and Theological locations. Termination ends the cycle of the existent Universe that had begun with the previous Creation. Thus with Initiation (the Creation) and Termination, the two main powers of God have been exercised and another cycle of existence has been completed.

22

GOD–AFTER THE END OF THE UNIVERSE

"Where nothing is done,
good order is universal."

(Tao Tê Ching)

For the most part, the examination of God AFTER the End of the Universe has not been given any real emphasis in most Religions. Most of Theology has been dominated by considerations involving only the existent Universe. Indeed, Theology concentrates directly on matters relating to Life, the Soul (or equivalent), and God. Only in the existent Universe are these important basic entities of Theology both identifiable and existent.

The major term here is existence. Existence defines the condition that something is. Only when something is or exists, is that something meaningful to the various aspects of conventional Theology. For it is said that "God exists." There can be no discussion nor any Theology if God does not exist. It can also be said that heaven exists and that the

219

Soul exists. Thus the key consideration of Theology has concentrated upon the mandatory condition that there must be existence.

But that which is said to exist, must also be cyclical (see Chapter 23). There is usually a beginning (creation) and an end (termination) that can be identified with all existent things. Even the existent Universe must follow these premises and eventually come to an end.

It is possible for the Universe to end in a variety of ways. It could do so by the completing of its cycle, in which case, further existence would be untenable. The end of the Universe could also be caused by some huge catastrophic event that could bring it rather quickly to its final termination at any time during its cycle after Creation. Whatever the way might be, the Universe must undergo Termination at some particular time. When this Termination does finally occur, it will produce a number of subsequent results that will have especial importance to Theology. Therefore, we shall now turn our attention to consider what this means to Theology and how this affects God.

The overall effect of Termination is to bring the cycle of existence of the Universe to a close. The existent Universe as well as its container (i.e., the name for how its substance is held, or expressed mathematically, the geometry of dimensions) will be totally ended so that everything that previously existed will be fully eliminated. So complete is the Termination, that nothing remains.

The prelude to Termination is Eschatology. When the various Scriptures are examined with respect to Eschatology, it will be noticed that there is much less treatment of this topic than is usually found with respect to most other Theological subjects. Eschatology represents one of the most difficult of all Theological concepts. For here, the existence of the Universe is ending and reverting back to its final condition of total Nothing. The realization and understanding of Nothing (as a full organized subject) is considered to be one of the three most difficult of all possible concepts (the other two being Time and God). Therefore, the reversion of Something to Nothing presents a severe challenge to comprehension, especially where this must be examined on such a huge scale.

The different Religions have examined this situation in various ways. Hinduism and Buddhism both have referred to Nirvana (literally meaning "to blow out" with respect to the flame of life) as the final desired state. In Hinduism, Nirvana additionally implies a reunion with Brahma. In Buddhism, an aspect of Nirvana involves the extinction or end of the individual existence, and the absorption or blending of the Soul into the Supreme Spirit. With both of these interpretations, the included Supreme Spirit or Being would be said to exist.

This condition of implied existence forms the key element for all further interpretation. For this means that we are dealing with the PHENOMENON OF GOD, which is an existent entity. The Soul is also an existent entity by definition (see Chapter 11). Existence can only be absorbed by existence. Therefore, the included aspect or presence of the Supreme Being must be existent. And so, we are dealing with the phenomenon of God, which is the manifestation of God in the existent Universe.

As existent entities, the phenomenon of God as well as all Souls will be completely eliminated at the final phase of the Termination of the Universe. The concepts of Eschatology, as stated in the various Scriptures, can only apply during the existence of the Universe. They can NOT apply after it. Thus Termination will even end all aspects of Eschatology.

There will be a number of major aspects associated with the conditions and situations found AFTER Termination. These can be stated as follows:

1. There is no possibility for existence of any kind.
2. There can be no container nor any geometrical dimensions.
3. There can be no heaven, hell, nor any other equivalent types of places or locations.
4. There can be no Souls, Spirits, nor any other aspects or remnants of Life.
5. There can be no formal existence of God.

It is important to realize that after Termination, there is no existence whatsoever. There can be no existence by definition. The existent Universe has been ended and by that ending, everything that was ever in it must cease to be.

Since there is no existence, there is nothing to support a container for existence. Thus there is no means for holding anything and there are no geometrical dimensions of any kind. This definite lack of a container provides further confirmation of the total cessation of the existent Universe.

With no place for anything, there can be no heaven nor hell nor anything in any way equivalent. Thus there is no place of any kind to put any Souls or Spirits, even if there were any of these during this particular period. However, there can be no Souls nor Spirits nor any other portions or remnants of life after final Termination.

As Termination occurs, the sequence for the ending of everything happens in exactly the reverse order in which it was originally created or developed. Thus the first thing created is the last to be terminated. Since the first creation in the Universe was God (see Chapter 6), the existence of God is the last thing terminated. This existence of God actually involves the concept of the phenomenon of God in the existent Universe. With the final and complete termination of existence, there is no place for any phenomenon, not even the one of God.

The period AFTER Termination will be exactly the same

as it was BEFORE Creation. There is no existent Universe, nor is any part of it even possible. Nothing exists. More precisely, the Concept of Nothing is identified. Therefore, the all-pervading situation is the non-existent Realm of Nothing, with its total lack of geometrical dimensions and with the complete absence of any kind of substance.

Although everything else is gone, it should be noted that the noumenon or reference or Soul of God remains separate and isolated in this Realm of Nothing. The basic identification of this reference of God is unaffected by any happening in the existent Universe, no matter what that happening might be. Thus neither the Creation nor the Termination, nor anything else associated in any way with the existent Universe, can have any effect upon the noumenon or reference of God.

This noumenon identification of God is said to occur within this Realm of Nothing. Only the term "identification" can be used at this point since there is no existence in the Realm of Nothing. Therefore it can never be said that anything "exists" there. There is just nothing there.

But at times it may be desirable for some reason to consider a particularly special something as being in some manner associated within this Realm of Nothing. In such an instance, that something would then be "identified" with this Realm and the examination and the subsequent development could proceed further. This directly applies to the Continuity Concept of God.

If God is to have any continuity outside of the existent Universe, then He must have some identification within this Realm of Nothing. Otherwise, God could not be perpetuated after the Termination of the existent Universe. This means that there must be some manifestation or representation of God in the Realm of Nothing. Thus there must be something there with which we can associate God.

The second important something within the Realm of

Nothing is the noumenon of Time (see Chapters 3 and 10). The initiation and continuity of everything is provided by the concept of Time (see the book of TIME).

Time initiates Change. It is through Change that the existent Universe derives its dynamic qualities and characteristics. It is the Noumenon of Time that can be said to reference all operations, functionings, happenings, and entities as they may occur in the existent Universe as well as in the non-existent Realm of Nothing. As such, this Noumenon of Time and the Soul of God exhibit identical properties and capabilities. Therefore, they can be said to be one and the same.

Thus we come to the final interpretation. God is and will always remain the reference of Theology. But it is the concept of Time that provides for the operational mechanism that references and initiates everything that ever was, is, or ever will be—no matter whether that everything (or any portion thereof) may be in either the existent Universe or the non-existent Realm of Nothing.

Thus we have the entelechy of the duality of God and Time. Each is identified with the other as being one and the same. God is the reference and the significance. Time is the means and the instrumentation. Together they form a coincident intrinsic combination that references, implements, and provides for the ultimate meaning.

Part VII

PERSPECTIVES IN THEOLOGY

23

CONCEPT OF THE REPEATING CYCLICAL UNIVERSE

*"The thing that hath been, it is that which shall
be;
and that which is done is that which shall be
done:
and there is no new thing under the sun."*
(The Bible, O.T., Ecclesiastes 1:9)

In the beginning there was the Creation. Thus it came to
be known that the Creation of the Universe was synonymous
with "The Beginning." For what was there before this?
Could anything have been there before this? Indecd, prior to
this special event, we have said that there was nothing. We
have called this situation the Realm of Nothing, or in mathematical terminology, the Realm of Zero. It was stated that
this Realm of Nothing was the prelude to Creation.

Yet we must question this further and ask whether there
was something else before this Beginning? Was there some
previous existence before our Universe? Is it possible that
there was another Universe before this one? And could
something else have existed even before that?

Although we are now considering the extreme depths of
the distant past, we can also speculate and question the future. It is said that some day our Universe will possibly come
to an end. But if that happens, will that end be final? Or will

something else, some further existence, follow our present Universe?

Questioning the past and the future can provide insight into the aspects of the present. One of the major conclusions disclosed by all the various discussions included herein is that the Universe is totally different from anything that could ever be imagined. Indeed, its substance, composition, and geometrical container are all well beyond anything that seemed revealed by the individual and combined perception of the senses. In fact, the senses have been completely inadequate to deal with anything beyond the immediacies of any presented apparent situation.

The Universe is much more than just its immediate substance, composition, and containing geometry. It also involves numerous functionings, interactions, and operations. That the Universe ever came into being is the greatest enigma of them all. For it is said that the Universe exists, and that there is a pattern to this existence.

The occurrences and the behavior of the operational patterns of the Universe are quite unusual. It is these patterns which are of especial interest since they can be applied to many other things. In a further sense, everything represents a smaller self-contained Universe in itself. Knowledge or principles derived from the overall Universe, can also be useful for the interpretation of many other things, such as the happenings of events and the derivation of thought (see Chapter 24). Therefore, let us now examine certain particular characteristics of the overall Universe.

With respect to its existence, the Universe has a number of aspects that warrant the consideration of its being cyclical. It has a beginning which starts with its Creation. It has an ending denoted by its Termination. In between, there are identifiable portions which exhibit the properties of growth and decay. Thus the aspects of a particular beginning, then growth, then decay, and finally a definite end—all are present to indicate that the Universe is cyclical.

Following the Creation are a number of specific steps and operations whose occurrences must take place in accordance with a specific sequential pattern. The aspects and the order of the events, things, and happenings that comprise the beginning sequential pattern of the Universe, are always the same. It can be shown (see the book of EXISTENCE) that the mathematical relationships for the beginning phase of the Universe are fixed and will always remain the same regardless of any possibilities or effects to the contrary. Thus no matter how else it might be considered or otherwise postulated, the Universe must always start in the same way and continue its development in a fixed manner.

It is of the highest importance to understand that, at the Moment of Creation, there was no possibility whatsoever for there to be a thinking process of any kind in operation. By definition, that which is called thinking requires that there be at least two or more geometric groups of dimensions available as a formal requirement to facilitate or enable the process. At the Moment of Creation, there are no dimensions at all. Therefore, there can be no thinking of any kind available to guide or vary the Creation and the immediately following beginning phase of the Universe. Thinking about something can allow for change in that something. However, when all capability for thinking is either prevented or excluded, there can be no change possible in any of the operations occurring during the beginning phase. Therefore these must always remain the same and thereby be in accordance with the basic Definition of Existence:

ANYTHING IS, BY VIRTUE OF ITS MEETING
THE DEFINITION OF ITS OWN EXISTENCE.

Thus the Universe is fixed in its development and operations in accordance with its own definition.

The process of existence is such that it will continue until it is terminated. When the Universe does undergo Termination, either at its natural end by cyclical completion or at some premature time by reason of some all consuming catastrophe, it would then cease to be. The consequence of this would be a reversion back to the Realm of Nothing. This situation would continue until the associated conditions of Creation were met. When these required initial conditions were right, then the event of Creation would again take place. The Universe would then begin again and would develop in exactly the same manner as before. Thus the Universe depends upon its definition to be, and the necessary initial conditions to begin. This leads to the conclusion that the Universe exhibits cyclical variations in its operations and has the propensity for repetition.

This inherent capability for repeating cyclical operations shows up in many things in the Universe. Especially the numerous forms of life show the same cyclical variations for each separate species in their activities relating to their spans of existence. Each species is characterized by similarities among their own kind which show relatively identical behavior and other functional patterns which repeat at prescribed points in their existence cycles. The extensive nature of these repeating cycles lends distinct support to the concept of the repeating cyclical Universe.

The Concept of the Repeating Cyclical Universe is further borne out by the Scriptures that are presented in the first four main sections of the New Testament of the Bible. These Scriptures are known as the Gospels According to (the Christian Saints) Matthew, Mark, Luke, and John. All of these are similar and tell about the life and teachings of Jesus. Yet each one has identifiable differences. The first three are so similar to each other that collectively they have been given the name of "Synoptic Gospels" (where Synoptic means—to see together).

The significance of presenting the same story four times appears to be an indication of a repeating aspect of the coming of Jesus. Especially prophecy and predestination are stressed. It is said in each Gospel that the prophets have foretold this coming. When Jesus does arrive, all the ensuing happenings appear to be preordained to occur in a fixed specific way leading to a particular purpose. "For Jesus knew from the beginning" (The Bible, N.T., John 6:64).

As this story of Jesus is repeated in each Gospel, there are variations among the presented points or details, but the main steps are always the same. The implication is that if the Universe ended and then began a new cycle, all would be as it was in the previous story or existence. In each new repeating existence cycle, Jesus would appear again during the same time period in the chronological sequence of developments and do just as He did before. Thus there would continue the predestined aspects of the Repeating Cyclical Universe.

Many things appear to indicate the possibility of the composite qualities of repetition and cyclical existences of the Universe and to substantiate them for use in a coordinated theory. Such additional interpretation of this concept can be provided by examining the related aspects of the existence of the Universe utilizing the capabilities of mathematics. This can be done by making use of the Equation of Existence that has been developed for presentation in the book of EXISTENCE. When the initial conditions of creation are placed into this equation, there is one and only one mathematical answer that can be obtained. This answer defines the first step in the creation of the Universe. No matter what approach may be used, the first step is always this particular resultant answer. The first creation (see Chapter 6) is always represented by this step with its associated operation, and nothing else

Once this first step in the creation of the Universe is concluded, the continuing process moves into a triple arrangement of separate binary patterns. Within the format presented in the book of EXISTENCE, everything which is said to exist is placed into the three separate categories of Energy (E), Life (L), and Matter (M). An individual mathematical model has been developed for each of these three and the combined results are referred to as the E-L-M Tabulations. Each of the associated mathematical models has binary characteristics. Thus after the first step of creation, the process branches out along three separate paths wherein each enters an individual binary pattern. The beginning portions of this overall process are diagrammatically represented in Figure 5.

As shown on this diagram, each step has associated with it a number of points. As the order number (S) of the steps increases, the number of points (P) also increases. The relationship to determine the number of points (P) included with any particular step (S) is (except for the first step):

$$P = 3 \times (2)^{S-2}$$

It will be seen that the "3" involves the three main branches of existence which are Energy (E), Life (L), and Matter (M). Each one of these branches increases in binary fashion by doubling with each step. Each step (S) represents a discrete separate change category which takes place in the orderly sequential development of the Universe. Each set of points (P) represent the various operations and happenings that are associated with each step.

The E-L-M Tabulations, developed and shown in the book of EXISTENCE, show the more detailed arrangements of the mathematical patterns in each of the E-L-M branches. Each of these E, L, and M Tabulations represents a detailed mathematical model that separately denotes Energy (E), Life (L), and Matter (M). These tabulations, as well as the step and points relationships, can be used in a variety of ways to produce a number of highly precise interpretations. These

232

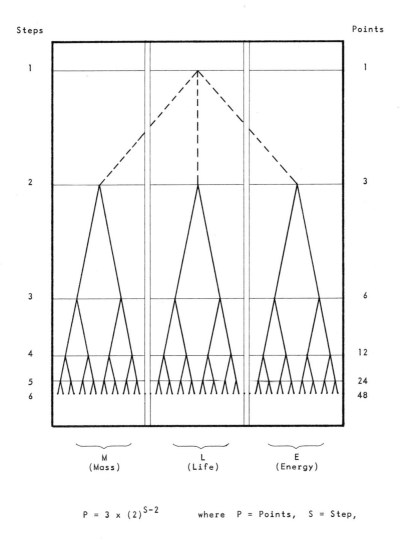

Steps				Points
1				1
2				3
3				6
4				12
5				24
6				48

M
(Mass)   (Life)   (Energy)
L   E

$$P = 3 \times (2)^{S-2} \quad \text{where} \quad P = \text{Points}, \quad S = \text{Step},$$

FIGURE 5 - THE BEGINNING OF THE STEPS
AND POINTS IN THE UNIVERSE

233

provide specific values and arrangements to the patterns of existence.

All this indicates a most definite order in the happenings and effects of the creation activities. No matter what approach is used to examine the associated activities, the order and arrangement of the included steps must remain exactly the same. For each new step to occur, the previous step must first be fully completed. This means that all points in any given step must be operationally completed before the overall process can move on. Under no circumstances can the process continue unless all previous steps are first completed. If any step presents difficulties such as to prevent its completion, the entire process must stop.

Under this orderly sequential predetermined step by step arrangement, it would appear that everything was arranged to happen on the basis of Predestination. While this is so for the steps, it is not so for the set of points that is associated with each step. Here the order for completing each set of points is not fixed. There is a certain freedom allowed in the completing of the points in each set. Depending upon the various factors and other associated conditions, almost any point may be started first with operations moving in some non-logic arrangement through the set until the completion of the step is effected. THUS FREE WILL IS ASSOCIATED WITH THE SET OF POINTS INCLUDED WITHIN A STEP, WHILE PREDESTINATION IS ASSOCIATED WITH THE STEP ITSELF.

With aspects of Predestination associated with the entire pattern of the steps, the entire system of steps works on a fixed preset pattern. If the pattern and its entire existence were to be destroyed and cease to be, there would be an inherent propensity for everything to start up again and proceed along the exact same pattern of steps as before. The only flexibility would be within the set of points associated with each step. But the overall steps themselves must remain precisely the same.

As is noted on the E-L-M Tabulations presented in the book of EXISTENCE, each tabulation has a definite mathematical end. This means that each group of steps must finally terminate. When this happens, the overall process comes to its end. TIME THEORY STATES THAT FOR SOMETHING TO EXIST, ITS EXISTENCE MUST CONTINUALLY BE RENEWED. As long as the transitions from step to step continue, the existence defined by the associated pattern will maintain itself intact. But once the pattern is finally completed, that existence must cease to be.

Thus the pattern of existence of the Universe must finally come to an end. With this end, the Universe will be destroyed. This destruction will continue until all trace is completely gone of that which was called the Universe. But the system has the propensity to start up again. Once it starts up, it must follow the exact prescribed pattern of steps that occurred before. This means that the Universe will follow a definite pattern in its existence. This pattern is cyclical and has the ability to repeat. Thus the conclusion is inferred that the Universe has had prior existences and will continue to have repeating similar existences extending indefinitely into the future.

24

THE HAPPENING OF THEOLOGICAL EVENTS (Why Things Happen)

"Is there any thing whereof it may be said, See, this is new? it hath been already of old time, which was before us."

(The Bible, O.T., Ecclesiastes 1:10)

There are some subtle characteristics of the Universe that allow for and augment its various particular functionings. The repeating cyclical qualities discussed in Chapter 23, point out the capabilities of the Universe to operate in certain fixed patterns. However, there are possible variations that can function within the framework of these fixed patterns to provide for change under specific circumstances. Thus the Universe has available for its use, composite sets of operations for both predetermined and changeable happenings.

Since almost anything can be considered a smaller Universe in itself, any information especially developed for the overall Universe will usually be applicable to most other things as well. Included in this group is the concept known as the "Happening of Events." This is the area that deals with the question of why anything happens as it does.

An identifiable situation that occurs as the result of a particular functioning, can be called an "event." A grouping of related functionings will represent a sequence or a "happening of events." This concept of a happening of events can be further described as a specific series of incidents, episodes, and occurrences that takes place between a particular initiation of activities and an associated conclusion. The concept accountable for the happening of events has aspects and relationships that are associated with the theory involved with the repeating cyclical Universe. From this duality of identification and operation, we can begin to examine such questions as:

Why do things happen as they do?
Why do we obtain our particular set of thoughts?

The theory of the repeating cyclical Universe leads to a number of unusual implications and possibilities. If the cycle of the Universe has occurred many times before our present one, then the associated happenings of the Universe can have had similar previous occurrences. By the Concept (see Chapter 23) of the Steps and Points (which represent an equivalence to Predestination and to Free Will respectively), the major categories (Steps) of happenings, events, and entities will *always* repeat. However, the circumstances (the Points) of how and why they repeat can have the ability to vary, which can definitely affect the way that they actually do occur. This means that although the main happenings that take place in the Universe must always be the same and occur in the same order during each separate existence cycle of the Universe, there could be different ways, means, and reasons associated with how each of these main happenings came into being. This would mean that a particular major aspect in history could have appeared in a different way in each separate previous Universe.

An example of this can be noted in the controversy that concerns itself with missing portions of the life of Jesus Christ. From the time that He was 12 to approximately 29 years of age, very little is known about the life of Jesus. The Bible notes that at the age of 12, Jesus debated in the Temple (Luke 2:42-46). After this episode, nothing more is provided until Jesus was full grown and beginning His career as a definite Holy Man at the age of about 29. What happened in-between is not really known, and has become the subject of much controversy.

One out of many possibilities is the story that Jesus travelled to India where He visited a number of monasteries to study. In this context, it is said that He became influenced by various concepts of Hinduism. Indeed, there are certain prominent similarities between Hinduism and Christianity. Both have a major Holy Trinity arrangement in their God structures. Hinduism has the Trimurti which consists of the God Trinity of Brahma (the Creator), Vishnu (the Preserver), and Shiva (or Siva, the Destroyer). Christianity has the Trinity involving the union (in one Godhead) of three divine entities which include the Father, the Son, and the Holy Ghost (or Spirit). It is interesting to note that the Sanscrit word "Trimurti" (three bodies or shapes) and the English word "Trinity" have similar meanings. In addition, both Theologies stipulate and accept the Hindu-originated concept of the "avatar," in which an extension of the Deity can and does come down to Earth and assumes an Earthly form in order to promote God's work.

Such similarities would tend to give credence to this story. Yet there are other possibilities that could explain the way that such similarities came about. Time Theory (see the book of TIME) suggests that similar happenings may occur at different places in the exact same format because they are synchronized to take place at the particular time of their initiation. Happenings, especially in thought or idea generation, occur because the associated conditions (the Steps) have reached certain levels which foster predestined specific operations. Thus with the appropriate conditions, the associated consequence can result in the same idea coming at the same time to two or more people who are separated from each other by distant geographic locations.

With respect to all this, there could be a number of explanations that could be developed and presented to deal with any happening. Indeed as research is continued, many new explanations could be derived and strong cases made for them by their adherents.

With a cyclically repeating Universe, ALL these situations may have actually occurred, with each specific happening taking place in a separate particular Universe. They would have occurred at the exact same period in the respective cycle of existence. Each of these separate occurrences could be considered as one of the POINTS involving the necessary tasks associated with each STEP (see Chapter 23). The purpose of the actual happening, was to fulfill the requirements of meeting the conditions for the particular STEP or category of the major overall situation.

Sometimes there are very dramatic divergences of opinion involving people of good faith in their interpretations of especially critical happenings. One of the major tenets of Christianity is that Jesus was crucified and died on the Cross, which was followed by the Resurrection. Yet another point of view has been presented wherein it is stated that Jesus was revived and actually lived on. Then He went to India where He lived out the remaining years of His life (see "Jesus Died in Kashmir" by Andreas Faber-Kaiser, published by Gordon & Cremonesi in London in 1977).

Though this controversy may be argued vehemently, the Concept of the Repeating Cyclical Universe allows for both possibilities. Each may have individually served to implement Christianity in its development in previous Universes.

The surrounding conditions (or Points) could have allowed for both (as well as other possibilities) to occur, each happening in a different previous Universe.

It is this possibility of variance in the order of the occurrence of the activities associated with the Points (or Free Will) that can account for the differences in opinion that take place in the thinking process. It is possible that no thought is ever original in the sense that it just comes about by itself. Rather each thought can be considered as the consequence of an arrangement, a special sequence of the available Points associated with a particular Step in the predetermined development of the Universe. Thus that which is called a "thought," can now be defined as a pattern arrangement of the Points associated with a specific Step in the Step-Point Concept of the Repeating Cyclical Universe.

It is these conditions of the Universe, as expressed through the Points, that provide for not only the happenings therein, but for the culmination of thought as well. These conditions, as well as their order of influence and application, provide the background for the Universe. If the same conditions repeat, then the same effects must result. This is like describing the phenomenon of Déjà Vu, where the individual becomes aware of a realization of having some prior knowledge of a presently occurring happening. The knowledge develops as a result of a particular ordering of the available Points. This ordering must be made from the AVAILABLE points, so that there is a limit on the number of the possible combinations and choices. Since selections from these choices represent Free Will, there is accordingly a limit on the extent of the total amount of Free Will possible.

Thus a thought represents one particular arrangement of the available Points. A different arrangement will represent a different thought. Two separate thoughts on the same subject in divergence to each other can represent a controversy. It is possible that, in a previous existence or cycle of a prior Universe, each happening or representative separate thought may have taken place. Thus a cyclical variation of the Universe can be considered as a cyclical variation of the ordered pattern arrangements of the available points.

Finally, there is a larger perspective to all this. CYCLICAL VARIATIONS PROVIDE FOR THE FREE WILL CAPABILITY FOR THINKING. It was shown in Chapter 14 that the major Theological reasons for the Creation of the Universe were to provide for the existence manifestations of God and to provide Him with the capability and necessary conditions for thinking. With cyclical variations of the Universe, there can be cyclical variations to these manifestations and to His thinking. Thus the cyclical variations allow for some measure of change and choice within the repeating framework involved with the continuity of God and the Universe.

25

DESCRIBING GOD

"I AM THAT I AM"
(The Bible, O.T., Exodus 3:14)

From all the foregoing derivations, analyses, and interpretations presented in the previous chapters, an overall perspective can now be developed to describe God. The information now available can be combined and organized to provide a composite presentation dealing with the actual aspects and description of God. Thus the concept of the Deity, the main subject of the devotion of the various Religions of the world, can now be singled out for proper attention and meaning.

When attempting to describe anything, it is important to note that, prior to doing anything else, the attendant conditions must be evaluated and taken into account. Any statement that is made about anything whatsoever, is valid only if it meets the requirements of its own associated conditions. The conditions associated with any something, form the

242

foundation upon which to build and explain that something. They take precedence over everything else. They must be fully available at the time of the particular happening, interaction, or entity or these subject things just can not exist nor operate in the prescribed or desired manner that is being presented by the statement that is under consideration.

For a train to go from one particular place to another, there must be railroad tracks providing the way between the two places. No matter how otherwise perfect the train may be, the train can not accomplish its desired journey if there is no track available. The tracks represent the associated conditions necessary before the train can perform the function of travelling.

For there to be a beverage known as coffee which can be consumed as an end objective, there must be suitable containers provided, such as a pot and cups, to implement and facilitate the included processing requirements. No matter what else is done or otherwise made available, there can be no coffee if there are no pots nor cups. Thus the pots and the cups form the very necessary conditions that provide for the existence and then the consumption of the coffee.

These examples illustrate priority considerations denoting the conditions that must be available to facilitate a desired situation. A desired situation or objective can only come about if the means are ALL present to allow for them. This requirement of the necessary supporting conditions to be present is so important that it takes priority over everything else. Everything is bound by its own conditions. Even God and His operations must comply. Thus when we attempt to finally describe God, we must consider this task in relation to the surrounding conditions that are associated with God.

In beginning our definition, we can say that God is a PROCESS representing a system of Life whose manifestations appear in a repeating cyclical Universe. Within this Universe, the phenomenon of the Holy Presence is created, developed, and then said to exist. Indeed the existence of God is contingent upon the existence of the Universe.

That which is known as God does not always exist. Without a Universe, there can be no existence of God. For the Universe provides the conditions necessary to facilitate the existence or the phenomenon of God.

Due to the two separate domains which include the Realm of Nothing and the existent Universe, there are TWO aspects of God which must be considered. The Realm of Nothing is a stable steady-state domain which is described as being non-existent, a situation that can be characterized as the direct opposite of existence. There are no and there can be no dimensions, nor the containing aspects usually developed by particular groups of dimensions. There can be no existence nor any possibility of any extension of existence. The Realm of Nothing can be considered as a non-existent point of which it can be said that there is nothing within and nothing outside. Yet this point and what it represents is available at all times. It is the reference of the Universe and all that will come into being. As such, an aspect of God is always identified with it.

This aspect that is identified in the Realm of Nothing is the Soul of God. It is the reference of everything and all that can ever be. But in its location within the Realm of Nothing, it is capable of nothing and it does nothing. It is like an operations center in limbo, just waiting. It is like a seed that is full of potential, that just waits for the necessary conditions to begin to allow it to start to develop and to ultimately bloom. It is truly a seed of destiny.

This Seed of Destiny comes into its own within the existent Universe. The Universe is created for the specific purpose of facilitating the process for the development of the phenomenon of God (see Chapter 14). As a manifested phenomenon, this representation of God in the Realm of Existence (i.e., the Universe) permits the doing and functioning of God to implement—"Thy Will be done" (The Bible, N.T., Matthew 6:10).

The practical implementation of God is accomplished in the existent Universe through that special category of existence which is known as "LIFE." THE ENTIRE SYSTEM OF LIFE MAKES UP THE COMPOSITE STRUCTURE OF GOD. All Life taken together is the totality of God. This is the structure of a Pantheistic God, where He is the single combined manifestation of all the multiple things in the Universe.

Depending upon the emphasis given to the different portions of the definition of God, aspects of Pantheism, Monotheism, Polytheism, and even Atheism can each be variously propounded and supported.

1. Pantheism (belief in a God whose manifestation is the sum total of each and every part in the Universe) is indicated since it can be said that God is actually composed of the entire structure of all Life including all other categories of supporting types of existence as well.

2. Monotheism (belief in one God) can be indicated since God can be said to involve one single system of the entire structure of all Life in the Universe.

3. Polytheism (belief in many Gods) can be indicated since the entire structure of the system of Life is actually composed of many separate Life-forms.

4. Atheism (belief in no God) can be supported by the Concept of the Zero Universe, which states that for all practical purposes, the Universe is essentially empty and devoid of all substance. This concept compares the amount of the actual substance that was created and developed in the Universe to the unimaginably immense volume of the size of the geometrical dimensions or container of the Universe. This size is so huge that the contents within are inconsequential, and thus can be considered as being zero. If for all practical purposes there is nothing in the existent Universe, and if by

245

definition there is nothing in the Realm of Nothing, then it can be argued that there is truly nothing that can be used to indicate or to imply that there is a God!

Thus it is that cases can be made for each of the four major categories of Religious belief which relate to the various concepts of God. The adherents of each belief reach their particular conclusion in accordance with the priority with which they rate and rank the included data associated with the overall definition of God. By taking one specific aspect and then emphasizing it above anything else, the particular category of Religious belief then becomes established.

In the final analyzation and interpretation, certain particular aspects do take priority over the others being considered. These relate to the existent Universe and include its geometry of existence as well as the other conditions, so that certain very definite conclusions can be drawn.

1. For God to be able to manifest Himself, there must be an existent Universe to provide the necessary environment and the conditions to allow His phenomenon to appear and to function.

2. God is always referred to as the "Living God" so that His manifestation within the existent Universe must be considered as a form of Life.

3. To provide God with all His capabilities and attributes requires the combined capabilities of ALL Life, so that God represents the entire system of Life in the Universe.

4. This system of Life stems from the first Creation in the Universe (see Chapter 6) which is the fountainhead or the primary manifestation of God.

5. This first Creation, by definition, is only a reference point geometrically, and actually represents the simplest of all Life-forms.

6. This first Creation can only indulge in the very simplest of tasks and is not capable of any thinking.

7. To increase Its capabilities, it is required that other Life-

forms be combined with It on a team-like basis to help with Its operations.

8. The total amount of the maximum complexity of the available types of Life-forms is directly proportional to the extent of the available number of geometrical dimensions in the Universe at the time of consideration.

9. The complexity or extent of the capability of God is directly related to the totality of the geometrical dimensions in the Universe.

10. The most important attribute of God is WISDOM.

11. The capability for wisdom is only obtained when the age of the Universe reaches the half-way point (Wisdom Point) in its existence cycle (see Chapters 10 and 20).

12. The included substances and the geometrical dimensions of the Universe follow mathematical binary relationships, and can double with the addition of each new dimensional group.

13. Since Wisdom is acquired after the half-way point of existence, it occurs after the realization of the occurrence of the final dimensional group.

14. This last dimensional group involves the conventional 3 dimensions of Euclidean geometry.

15. The Holy Presence will be manifested in the last dimensional group of the multi-dimensional existent Universe, by the physical presences of the existing Life-forms. These collectively will make up the final extension of God and provide for the phenomenon of His work.

16. The self-realization of God will occur from and through the First Creation. This will include all Life onward to and through the final dominant Life-form.

17. At the most dominant position of the structure or chain of the overall Life system will be the Life-form with the greatest intelligence.

18. God will realize His most important attribute—WISDOM, through the most dominant form of Life.

19. The most dominant Life-form on Earth is Man.

20. Therefore, using the Alpha and Omega Concept (The Bible, N.T., Revelation 22:13), the Wisdom of God will be actualized through Man (at least on Earth).

Thus is God a dualism that is referenced in the non-existent Realm of Nothing and actually manifested in the existent Universe. This means that the noumenon or Soul of God (see Chapter 12) is always in the Realm of Nothing, while His phenomenon or Holy Presence is manifested in the Universe on a repeating cyclical basis. The reference (noumenon) of God is fixed and unchangeable while His manifestations (phenomena) occur in direct accordance with the developments and stages associated with the ever changing Universe.

As a further interpretation, God can be described in a symbolic comparison with a biological process that develops a beautiful flower as its end product. Like the reference or Soul of God that lies inactive in the Realm of Nothing prior to the Initial Creation of the Universe, prior to the beginning of the plant, everything that is or ever will be lies dormant in a seed. The seed can be considered as a point or reference of the potential that ultimately can come into being. Like the Soul of God, the seed can remain in this dormant or latent state in which nothing can or will happen to it. But if and when this seed is subjected to those very special initial conditions that can vitalize it from its quiescent static situation to begin its dynamic operations, then and there it will experience its Moment of Creation.

Once the process is started, the seed will have its functions initiated. It will follow a series of predetermined operations that will lead inexorably to a final purpose (unless prematurely interrupted by some catastrophic event and conclusion). With the proper conditions provided and maintained, the seed (like the Universe) will start to grow into its particular structure. During its first phase, the physical manifestations of the developing plant will be relatively small and inconsequential. As the growth cycle continues, its size and capabilities will increase.

It will take a certain finite amount of time to reach each portion of the included growth or development cycle. Nothing can just happen instantaneously no matter whether it is the plant, the Universe, or God that is involved.

Finally, the plant will attain that important desired portion of its development cycle when it can produce a beautiful radiant flower. The achievement of this moment will serve and justify its entire existence. Indeed, the achievement of its ultimate purpose gives meaning to the entire process and credence for its total being.

Like the brief blooming of a flower that gives the entire process of the plant its moment of glory, so is it the manifestation of God that justifies the Universe and gives it its totality of meaning and purpose. For God is a process whose manifestation begins at the Moment of Creation and continues through the development of the Universe. The achievement of wisdom for God, is like the blooming of the flower is to the plant. It is the continuing striving for an end purpose that provides meaning for the process.

BUT THE PROCESS IS A NEVER ENDING ONE AND MUST BE REPEATED AGAIN AND AGAIN. THUS THERE IS A CONTINUITY OF PURPOSE, PROCESS, AND BEING THAT MUST GO ON IN PERPETUITY. SUCH IS THE RELATIONSHIP BETWEEN GOD AND THE UNIVERSE.

26

THE DEVELOPMENT OF GOD
IN THE UNIVERSE

"Now we have received,
not the spirit of the world,
but the spirit which is of God;
that we might know the things
that are freely given to us of God."
(The Bible, N.T., 1 Corinthians 2:12)

In the occurrence of things and events, nothing just happens immediately. Rather, there are usually distinct stages of development associated with everything. When anything comes into existence, it does so in a discrete series of steps whose aspects and happenings are directly identifiable in time.

Since God can not function within the non-existent Realm of Nothing due to the lack of the necessary environment and supporting conditions, the manifestation of the phenomenon of God can only occur in the existent Universe. The extent of such a manifestation must necessarily be limited by the availability of the means of implementing it. When the Universe is fully developed, it can provide for the required means, conditions, and environment to facilitate the functionings of God. But even the Universe itself does not come about immediately. Instead it takes time to develop. This development proceeds in definite stages that take place in specifically prescribed sequences after Creation. Since the development of God is dependent upon the development of the Universe, this means that the manifestations of God will also take time to occur and these will take place in stages. Even perfection takes a certain amount of time. Thus the manifestations of the aspects and capabilities of God will be directly related to, and also limited by, the advance of the sequential developments in the existent Universe.

From His definition and identification, God can be considered as consisting of two separate parts. These include the Soul (or reference) and the Manifestation (or presence) of God. The Soul is represented as the noumenon (what God IS) and has been identified as being in the Realm of Nothing (see Chapter 12). The Manifestation is represented as the phenomenon (what God DOES) and has been identified with the existent Universe. The Realm of Nothing, as the name implies, allows nothing to happen. Therefore, the manifestation of almost all activity associated with God is directed to the existent Universe. But before such activities can be facilitated, the Universe must be ready.

It is important to realize that nothing can be done unless the conditions are available and conducive for the desired happenings. Especially, complex happenings require complex supporting conditions. It takes time for complex conditions to come about. Thus there is a delay or transition time involved before many of the vital functionings of God can be put into effect. Even God can not function in certain ways unless the means are fully available to allow and promote such functioning.

Especially thinking and wisdom are included in this concept. Wisdom can not occur unless there is the capability for thinking. Thinking can not be done unless there is a multi-dimensional geometrical structuring available, such as is eventually found in the Universe. But especially this structuring takes time, so that there is usually a significant delay that must be considered and taken into account.

When all this is examined, we get a perspective of God that is set against the background of a developing Universe. From all the associated considerations, the various pertinent stages and included times can be determined and tabulated. The results of this are outlined and presented in chart form in Figure 6.

On this Theological-Time Chart of the Universe, the information representing the time in years associated with the main developments in the Universe, was obtained from Chapter 20. Here it was determined that the half-way point of the existence cycle of the Universe was equal to 12 billion years. It was disclosed that this half-way point in time occurred approximately 2,500 years ago. For the total period of a maximum complete span of existence for the entire Universe, the associated time involved would be double the half-way value, or 24 billion years.

Since the major mathematical proportions associated with the priority happenings of the Universe have already been established (see Chapter 10), the time equivalence in years can readily be determined by multiplying each of these proportions by 24 billion. For the Creation of the Earth, Geological estimations show that this event took place some 4 billion years ago (see Chapter 20). Since the half-way point of existence of the entire Universe has been set at 12 billion years, then the Creation of the Earth occurred at the Universe age of 8 billion years. Due to the fact that the 12 billion year value is considered as being the mid-way point for not only the Universe but the Earth as well, this consideration places the estimate for the termination of the existence span of the Earth at the 16 billion year point.

The capabilities for the functioning of God are directly associated with the development of the Universe. The most

FIGURE 6 - TABULATION OF THE DEVELOPMENT OF GOD

REF. NO.	TOTAL INTO Existence Cycle Years *	TOTAL INTO Existence Cycle Prop. **	HAPPENING	STATUS OF GOD	CHAPTER PRESENTED
1	0	0	Prior to Creation	Dormant in Realm of Nothing	2, 3, 12, 13, 29.
2	0	0	Initial Creation	Beginning of Existence	2, 4, 6, 7, 14, 15, 25.
3				First Phase of Development	5, 14.
4	3	1/8	SEX POINT, Thinking Point	Organized Thinking Begins	9, 23, 24.
5				Development	
6	8	1/3	Creation of the Earth	of	9, 10.
7				Thinking	
8	12	1/2	WISDOM POINT	Wisdom Begins	10, 20.
9				Wisdom	2, 9, 10, 14, 15, 16, 20, 25.
10	16	2/3	Termination of the Earth	in	2, 9, 10, 14, 15, 16, 20, 25.
11				Operation	2, 9, 10, 14, 15, 16, 20, 25.
12	21	7/8	TERMINATION PHASE POINT	Termination Begins	21, 22.
13				General Reversal of Existence	22.
14	24	1	Termination of the Universe	Final End of Existence	22.
15	0	0	After the Termination and Prior to Next Creation	Dormant in Realm of Nothing	25, 29, 30.

* Billions   ** Proportion

important attribute of God is WISDOM. The pre-requisite of wisdom is THINKING. Thinking is an activity that, like all others, requires certain basic conditions to be available before it can be performed. These conditions are never available within the Realm of Nothing, so thinking can never be performed there. These conditions do become available in the existent Universe, but not immediately after Creation. Rather it takes a certain amount of time and development before they can actually come about.

For the first 3 billion years after Creation, the geometrical dimensions (among other things) were being developed to the point where they could allow for the process of thinking to be performed. No really directed thinking could be done during this first period simply because the environment had not sufficiently developed to the point where organized thinking could be properly handled. Therefore, mature or directed thinking could not be performed during this initial period. This first stage of the Universe (corresponding to 1/8 of the total time span of existence) can be considered as a time of immaturity. It can be said that it was a time of thinking immaturity for God. Thus it was that, once initiated at Creation, the development of the Universe proceeded by DEFINITION along the prescribed aspects indicative of Pre-destination. It certainly was not under any organized thinking control that can be attributable to God.

The capability to perform useful thinking was acquired by God when the Universe was 3 billion years into its existence cycle. From here (the 1/8 point) to an age of 12 billion years (the 1/2 point), the thinking capability of God developed on a continually increasing basis in direct proportion and association with the development of the Universe. This 1/2 point is also the location in time where we can identify wisdom with the developed thinking process of God (see Chapters 10 and 20).

During this 1/8 to 1/2 span of existence, the Earth was

created at approximately the 1/3 point. Although the Creation and initial development of the Universe could not have been under the knowing control of God, the situation involving the Earth is totally different. The creation and initial development of the Earth occurred during the period of God which is definitely characterized by His capability for active mature thinking. Therefore the Religious statements cited in various scriptures such as "—God created the heaven and the earth" (The Bible, O.T., Genesis 1:1) are confirmed by the mathematics of Theology and Time.

For the inhabitants of the Earth, the most important part of the Universal Cycle of Existence is from the 1/2 to the 2/3 point. This is 1/6 of the total cycle (from 12 billion to 16 billion years). It represents that particular portion of existence where wisdom begins, to the estimated termination of the Earth. This is a period of potential wisdom for both God as well as Man. For God, this period represents the most important part of His operational existence or phenomenon cycle. It is during this time that His potential for good work reaches its highest capability.

It should be remembered that there is a most definite similarity between the operations of God, Man, and the Universe. Many times we have stressed the aspects of the Universe during our discussions. Whatever concepts apply to the overall Universe can usually be applied to other complete operational systems as well. Man (as well as other forms of Life) can be said to represent a Universe. God is dependent upon the Universe and its environmental conditions in order to perform His functions. Thus it can be considered that almost all the concepts developed for the overall Universe, can also be applied to God and to Man. That is why so much emphasis has been placed upon the discussions of the Universe.

Thus it is possible to identify this 1/6 proportional span (from the 1/2 to the 2/3 points), developed primarily from concepts related to the Earth and the Universe, also to relationships dealing with Man. This single period from the 1/2 to the 2/3 point during each Life represents the most important potential productive portion for each individual person. It begins approximately at the half-way point of each person's total span of life. It is here where Man's thinking potential reaches its highest capabilities to the point where that which is called "Wisdom" may occur. Once such wisdom is achieved and set into operation, it can continue to at least the 2/3 point. Often it will easily exceed past this and continue on for quite some time. Thus it is that the capability for wisdom develops during the zone included between the 1/2 and 2/3 points of the existence cycle of Man.

Moving from the 1/2 (Wisdom Point) to the 7/8 position (the beginning of Termination for the Universe), is a period characterized by the capability for the very highest level of thinking for God. It is interesting to note that it is during this period that the Earth is scheduled for termination (at the 2/3 point). It could be inferred that God, in His wisdom, exercised His power of termination to cause the destruction of the Earth (which is estimated to take place at approximately 16 billion years into the Universe cycle of existence).

Finally the 7/8 point is reached and Termination is initiated at 21 billion years. During the next 3 billion years, the Universe deteriorates and reverts back toward its original beginning in the exact opposite manner to its development. At the age of 24 billion years, the Universe is estimated to complete its total existence cycle and thereby end. With Termination, the manifestation of God in the existent Universe also comes to an end.

With everything reversing, the capabilities for thinking by God have also been diminishing. Finally with all His thinking capabilities gone, the last thing in the Universe stands alone and represents the culmination of the once mighty Universe. With the end of the Universe, comes the end of the development process of the Universe and to the totality of the cycle of existence.

Thus it is that the development of the phenomenon of God is directly associated with the corresponding development of the existent Universe. For the existent manifestation of God with all His capabilities requires that there be a Universe to provide the means to implement this special situation. It is for this purpose that the main Theological reason for the Creation of the Universe (see Chapter 14) is directed to facilitate the phenomenon of God. Thus it is that the hidden Soul of God expresses itself by manifesting the Holy Presence in and through the existent Universe.

27

EVIL

". . . your eyes shall be opened, and ye shall be as gods, knowing good and evil."
(The Bible, O.T., Genesis 3:5)

WHY? Why is there evil in the Universe? There is nothing in the God-given Universe that actually allows for evil. In all the discussions of Theology presented herein, the subject of evil has never been mentioned. Yet there is evil in the Universe. To what can we attribute it? For evil is the very antithesis of God and Theology. As such, it should have no possibility of originating in anything directly associated with God. Certainly God would not create evil. Since it was God who created the Universe, evil should not be. But it is. From where did it originate? If the source of evil can not be identified with any of the major Theological concepts, then this "notable omission" must have special significance. If that which is known as evil can not be identified with God or the Universe, then it must be associated with something else. This something else will be shown to be a completely sepa-

258

rate operating system (to be named the "Eaverse," pronounced ee-averse) which is part of the super ordered structure that also includes that which is called the Universe. This super structure is known as the "COSMOS" and can also be named the "ESAN."

Ordinarily when we think of the word "evil," we think of it in association with its conjugate word of "good." For good and evil are opposites and are usually considered as being relative terms. If we were to categorize all concepts into just two groups representing good and evil, and then somehow eliminate the "evil" group, we would be left only with those things which we call "good." But there would be gradations in this group of good, so those items in the lesser strata or rank might conceivably be considered as being bad or perhaps evil in themselves. However, it is just not possible to eliminate or dispense with evil. The Concepts of Good and Evil can each be identified with a completely separate structured system that accounts for its respective operations. The general concept of Good is associated with the existent Universe, while the general concept of Evil is now identified with an alter-universe hereinafter to be called the "Eaverse." Together, the existent Universe and the Eaverse represent parts of the ultimate all-encompassing super-structure that is called the "Cosmos."

Evil has manifested itself an endless number of times in a variety of forms and devastating effects. Perhaps the most terrible example in this century has been the knowing and deliberate organized slaughter of six million people of the Jewish faith, whose deaths were diabolically brought about on a mass basis by the perverse German Nazis under Hitler during the years of 1933 through 1945. As is characteristic of evil, it appears never to be fulfilled or ended, but rather it always tends to go on and on. In addition to the six million Jews, five million people of other faiths or politics who opposed the Nazis were also methodically slaughtered. All told, more than 55 million people were killed in the Second World War, as a horrible cataclysmic result of the ensuing evil.

Of the many such examples that could be cited in history, two are of especial significance. Each of these involves the destruction of an entire Religion knowingly and deliberately by another Religion. Almost all the followers of Zoroastrianism were put to the sword in a "Holy" crusade by the ravaging hordes of Islam, acting in the name of Allah, the compassionate! Similarly followers of Catholicism acting supposedly in the name of Jesus Christ, who is reputed to have said "turn the other cheek," destroyed Manichaeism in its entirety including all the people, books, documents, and all known relics! These acts of utter destruction represent evil in its most horrible form.

The fact that the responsibilities for these holocausts are acts done under the guise of Religion is particularly important. The use of these two examples is a means to illustrate the extent to which evil can go. If any Religion which extols the virtues of goodness can itself somehow engage in acts of indescribable horror, then it can be realized that anything can be made subject to the forces and effects of evil. Thus it can be seen that almost any individual or group of people, at some specific time and under some combination of unique circumstances, can indulge themselves and engage in a variety of almost unlimited acts of evil. This would also include individuals and organizations who usually act in good faith and in exemplary methods of conduct.

The two Religions that were destroyed, Zoroastrianism and Manichaeism, each possessed a very unusual feature that exceeded that found in any other Religion. Each dealt with the Concept of Evil in an advanced formal organized manner. Each provided interpretations into the subject of Evil that were well beyond anything else ever before available. It is an interesting commentary to note that these were the two Religions that were specifically singled out for total destruction. It was almost as if Evil had a mind of its own and was determined to make sure that it would remain in complete obscurity so that it could be unimpeded in its nefarious work.

In their own right, Zoroastrianism and Manichaeism each had their special relationships with respect to the other religions. All seven of the world's major religions had their origin in just one continent—Asia. Zoroastrianism was of significant size and influence so that it could be ranked and included among this major group of religions. It was also geographically located in the boundary zone separating the Eastern from the Western Religions. Judaism, Christianity, and Islam were in the west while Hinduism, Buddhism, and the Oriental Religions were in the east. Monotheistic concepts of God were dominant in the west, while essentially Polytheism was the dominant theological category in the east.

In between these eastern and western religions was found Zorastrianism with its concepts of TWO sets of Gods, where one represented good while the other represented evil. The evil God (Ahriman) was in continual conflict with the good God (Ahura Mazda). This persisting struggle in Zoroastrianism was one in which the outcome could not be decided or known beforehand. The Earth is seen as the battleground. Each God is actively engaged in enlisting as many people into His service as possible. Evil is characterized by being in constant operation wherein it ceaselessly strives for dominant resulting effects by outright activities involving challenging, combining, intertwining, and interacting with the available Good functionings. Thus Zoroastrianism considers Evil as something completely separate and apart from Good.

From a Theological point of view, it is said that God created the Universe. It is also said that God is good and that all His work is good. Therefore the Universe must be considered to be essentially good. If the concept of Evil is separate from

261

God and the Universe, then its origin must lie somewhere outside the Realm of God and the boundaries of the Universe. This is the implication suggested by Zoroastrianism and which is a most important inference of Theology.

The separation of Evil from the Good is further expounded by Manichaeism. Although Manichaeism obtained a number of its ideas from Zoroastrianism, it developed many of its own original ideas to deal with the Concept of Evil. Indeed the Cosmology of Manichaeism is perhaps the most developed and the most complete treatment that is offered by any Religion. The teachings of Mani (or Manes) separate and examine good (Light, God, and the Soul) in terms of its contrast with evil (Darkness, Satan, and the physical Body). Well before Creation, the situation is proposed by Mani of the God of Light looking down upon His dominion when He notices a dark top of a mountain representing the domain of Evil protruding up through the light clouds near the horizon. The God of Light creates a son, Gayomart, modelled as a forerunner of what is eventually to become the idea and the being of Man. Gayomart is armed with the five basic elements of light, ether, wind, water, and fire which are also of fundamental importance to Hinduism and Zoroastrianism. However, when he enters the dark mountain, the demons of darkness prove too strong for him. These demons attack and devour all five of the basic elements. In order to save Gayomart, the God of Light has to create a second champion who is Mithra, the power of the Sun. Mithra rescues what is left of Gayomart who is now totally naked and devoid of his five basic elements. To make Gayomart whole again, the God of Light creates the Universe using the bodies of the demons who have been slain by Mithra, so that the five basic elements may eventually be freed to return to the Godhead again. Since the demons were evil, the substance and the content of the Universe must be considered evil and satanic. Thus Manichaeism introduces the origin of evil as being outside the Universe and concludes that all matter and people are tainted by evil!

Especially, the human being is considered as being basically evil. Manichaeism states that to counter the maneuvers of the God of Light, the God of Darkness created Man in the person of Adam. Thus Manichaeism identifies the first man as being evil. Christianity makes the same assertion. Christianity states that evil as "sin" by Adam came—"by one man sin entered into the world" (The Bible, N.T., Romans 5:12). Evil in the physical being of man is further confirmed by the Christian Apostle, Paul, who states, ". . . I know that in me (that is, in my flesh) dwelleth no good thing" (The Bible, N.T., Romans 7:18). Thus Christianity and Manichaeism both identify that evil is associated with the human being right from the beginning. The source of this evil is considered to be Satan or the God of Darkness. Only the responsibility for the creation of Man is stated in contrast. Christianity maintains that Man was created by the good God as originally presented in the Judaic Theology, while Manichaeism states that it was the evil Satan that created Man. Manichaeism further states that Jesus was the third major extension of the Godhead (after Gayomart and Mithra) that was created by the God of Light to help in His struggle with the God of Darkness.

The symbolism of all this is of especial importance. Good and Evil have been presented as being contrasting entities which are separated from each other, at least with respect to their included origins. Good is associated with God, and with His created Universe. Therefore it would appear that the origin of Evil must lie somewhere outside of and beyond the confines of the existent Universe. To examine this possibility, we now turn to concepts already developed in the book of EXISTENCE.

263

When the mathematics of existence are examined, it was found that out of the total theoretical mathematical range of 0 to 100%, the substance which makes up the existent Universe accounts for less than 40% of the possible whole amount. This is located in the top portion of the range (i.e.– from the 60% to the 100% positions). This means that that which is said to exist, does so in the top 40% portion of the theoretical mathematical range of the totality of everything. This top portion thus accounts for all the Energy (E), Life (L), and Matter (M) of the Universe which are precisely defined in the E-L-M Tabulations which were developed in the book of EXISTENCE.

With only the top 40% of the total mathematical range of everything identified, no accounting has been made of the lower 60%. When only the Universe was considered, there was no need to pay any attention to this unaccounted-for range. But now the Concept of Evil suggests that something else lies hidden there. It is stated that something identified by the symbolism of Evil is located in this lower portion of the mathematical range of totality. If it is in this region, the next step is to locate exactly where it is and then determine the extent of its mathematical range.

It should be most obvious that the first place to begin to mathematically determine Evil is with the mathematical elimination of God. From a Theological point of view, God represents the good in the Universe. If we were to theoretically eliminate God, then what would be left would essentially be the representation of Evil. Therefore as a first step, we shall subtract the mathematical value associated with God from the totality of everything and use the remainder as a mathematical value of Evil.

The mathematical value associated with God has been determined to be 3/4 in Chapters 6 and 7. The totality of everything is equal to a value of "1," since the whole is equal to the sum of all its parts and there is nothing greater than the whole. Thus

The Whole	–	God	=	Evil
1	–	3/4	=	1/4

This proportion or value of 1/4 is associated with part of a range of numbers which shall be identified with the Concept of Evil. An important aspect of this mathematical Range of Evil is that it must lie OUTSIDE of the mathematical range that is associated with the Universe. Although the effects of Evil can be manifested within the Universe, its source could never be considered as originating in something created by God. Therefore, the numbers or values used to represent Evil will be other than those representing the existent Universe.

The existent Universe can be mathematically defined as appearing within a range of proportions or numbers that range from 0.6000 to 1.0000 in value (see the book of EXIS-TENCE). This means that the symbolism of the Universe occupies the upper portion of the total 0 to 1 mathematical range. When the mathematical value associated with God (0.7500) was subtracted from "1" to derive the first number representing Evil, the value of "1" referred to the very top limit of the 0-to-1 range. Since the upper limit (1) of the Universe (which is assessed as being "Good") was used to reference the first calculation, the result of "1/4" must accordingly be the upper limit of the mathematical range of Evil.

When the upper limiting value of the range of Evil is compared to the corresponding upper limiting value of the range of Good (i.e.- 1/4 to 1), the resulting ratio has a value of 1/4. This ratio can now be applied to the lower limiting value of the range of Good to determine the lower limiting value of the range of Evil. Accordingly:

$$1/4 \times 0.60000 = 0.1500$$

This ratio of "1/4" can be further used to obtain the mean center value of the Range of Evil by multiplying it by the corresponding value of the Range of Good. Accordingly:

$$1/4 \times 0.7500 = 0.1875$$

A tabulation of the Upper, Center, and Lower values of the mathematical Range of Evil is presented in Figure 7.

LOCATION	VALUE
Upper	.2500
Center	.1875
Lower	.1500

FIGURE 7 - THE MATHEMATICAL
RANGE OF EVIL

Now for some comments on this concept of the Mathematical Range of Evil. From a mathematical perspective, the entire numerical Range of Evil (0.1500 to 0.2500) lies completely outside of the range of Good which is symbolic of the existent Universe (0.6000 to 1.0000). The Range of Good is four times greater than the Range of Evil (0.4 as compared to 0.1 respectively).

The Theological implications and inferences that can be developed with respect to the mathematical ranges of Good and Evil are especially thought provoking. The energy called "Light" is considered to be good in both Zoroastrianism and Manichaeism where, in each Religion, Light is associated with the Good God. In the Judaic Scriptures of the Old Testament of the Holy Bible (which are also used to reference the Theology of Christianity and Islam), it is stated that—

"And God saw the light, that it was good:"
(The Bible, O.T., Genesis 1:4)

Thus at least five Religions subscribe to the concept that Light is associated with Good.

When a multi-dimensional geometrical analysis is performed on light energy, it can be shown that there is no possibility whatsoever for any of the numbers included in the entire Range of Evil to ever appear in any part of the mathematical series function associated with light. If they could appear, they would do so in the Second geometrical group (which shows up in the second place in the mathematics of the series function). However, for light or any other Energy (E), the usual place for the Second Group mathematical representation is always empty. There can be no numbers of any kind in the usual Second place and certainly none of those associated with the Range of Evil. Since light never has any Evil associated with it, it must be deemed as being Good, which is the conclusion stated in Scriptures.

267

For Matter or Life, the situation is entirely different. Manichaeism specifies that Matter and Man are both tainted by Evil. Concerning Matter, the Holy Bible states—

". . . cursed is the ground"
                                    (The Bible, O.T., Genesis 3:17)

Concerning Man, the Holy Bible states in two places—

". . . ye were the servants of sin"
                                    (The Bible, N.T., Romans 6:17,20)

When a multi-dimensional geometrical analysis is performed on Matter (M) and Life (L) (see the book of EXISTENCE), it can be shown that the mathematics of the Range of Evil can and do enter into the calculations for the Second geometrical group of dimensions. These representative numerical values associated with the Concept of Evil are most definitely present in the included mathematical functions. Thus aspects of Evil must be considered as being part of both Matter and Life.

Concerning the Concept of Life, the Devil (or Satan) is usually noted with respect to His designs upon the Soul. Within Theology, both God and the Devil are primarily interested in the human Soul. The human Soul has a center mathematical value of approximately 0.196 (see the book of LIFE). This value is derived for the Second Group of geometrical dimensions included within the multi-dimensional structural system associated with Man. This value also happens to fall within the mathematical Range of Evil. It should be noted that nowhere in any Scriptures of any Religion is the Devil ever interested in the physical body of Man. Rather, the only interest is with obtaining control and power over the Soul of Man. Indeed, the mathematics of the physi-

268

cal body of Man can not fit into the Range of Evil. Only the mathematics of the Soul of Man can match the included numerical values of the Range of Evil. This means that the Soul of Man is susceptible to the aspects of Evil and it is in the Soul that evil is developed.

The numerical values of the extension of Matter in the Second Dimensional Group range from 0.!500 to 0.1667 and fall right into the lower portion of the Range of Evil (see the book of EXISTENCE). Thus it can be seen that both Matter (M) and Life (L) have aspects that are conducive for operations associated with the Concept of Evil.

The Concept of Evil represents the most critical challenge in all of Theology. Evil is something that is separate and apart from God and all His creations. The effects and happenings of Evil are not under the control of God. Indeed, it appears that there is no possibility whatsoever for God to knowingly affect the happenings of Evil.

The teachings and concepts concerning Evil as advanced by both Zoroaster and Manes appear to be correct and to have special significance. Good and Evil represent distinct and individual things. They have separate origins, each in a location that is apart from the other. Each origin is such that it always remains unaffected by any influences exerted by the other. Although their origins are relatively inviolate, when they function in a common medium they can each interact with and affect the other.

The domain of the existent Universe represents a common medium in which Good and Evil can both operate and influence the other. In Zoroastrianism, it is stated that the Earth is the battleground where the forces that have been recruited and enlisted on the two opposing sides of Good and Evil will join in battle and fight it out to the final outcome, whatever that may be.

The problem concerning Evil becomes most emphatic in

the monotheistic Religions of western Asia. Indeed, these Religions (Judaism, Christianity, and Islam) all are hard-pressed to deal with Evil. With one supreme God, it would appear that He should be dominant over everything, and therefore, He should be able to totally eliminate all aspects of Evil. Yet Evil remains as a significant power with which to reckon. While symbolic devices and rationalizations are used to explain away Evil (such as Job in the Old Testament of the Bible), all such attempts are never really successful. Evil and its effects always remain and in doing so, they exert considerable influence. Even an all-powerful God can not manage to dispel Evil.

If the supreme God can not destroy Evil, then it must involve something that is outside His domain and beyond His capabilities. But if it is not in His domain, then its origin or location must be somewhere outside the Universe, for the entire Universe is the domain of God! Thus this gives rise to the possibility that there is something else besides the Universe in the general order of things.

The symbolism of the Concept of Evil leads inexorably to the conclusion that there is something else occurring and functioning outside of the boundaries of the Universe. Since the Universe can be described as a system, process, or operating structure, that something else must be some kind of a concurrent operating system. It has already been defined in an outline mathematical way. It has a presence and a set of operations that are independent of those of the Universe.

In other words, there is another universe beyond the present one. This extra universe has many of the major characteristics that are associated with the main one. It can be described as a system. It can be defined in mathematical terms. It is a composite operations-oriented structure that can function on its own. Some of these operations can extend outward beyond the boundary confines that enclosed this system and then exert influence and cause effects in other

270

separate systems. The name given to this separate additional universe is the "Eaverse."

If there is one additional structural system, then there is a distinct possibility that there can be others. This composite of the Universe, the Eaverse, and any other such system is called the "Cosmos."

The implications of the Concept of Evil are as follows. THE SOURCE OF ALL EVIL LIES OUTSIDE OF THE UNIVERSE. It is traceable to a separate system or structure that is separate and essentially independent of the Universe. This separate system is totally apart from God and any vestige or extension of His control. God has no responsibility for, nor power over, Evil and its origins.

The mathematics that can be used to define the Range of Evil show that it has relationships similar to those functions occurring in the Second Dimensional Group for Matter and Life in the existent Universe. Since these characteristics match each other, these provide a mechanism through which Evil can enter and influence happenings and entities in the Universe. Thus when Manes stated his Theological pronouncement that Matter and Man are tainted with Evil, his conclusions are borne out by the included mathematics. As further confirmation, those functions just described for Matter and Life are NOT present for any Energy. Thus Evil can never affect Energy directly so that the Light associated with Ahura Mazda of Zoroastrianism (and later with Manichaeism), always remains pure and Good! That Energy is Good is further confirmed in Christianity where God is referred to as the "the Father of lights" (The Bible, N.T., James 1:17).

Each of the geometries associated with the mathematical structure of the Universe and of the Eaverse can symbolically be represented by the form of a pyramid. At the top or summit of this pyramid is the pinnacle or apex point. This is the most important and the most critical point in the entire structure. In the included mathematics, this apex represents the very first thing that is developed. After and from this point, everything else stems. This is the fountainhead or source from which everything else follows.

From the mathematical structure of the Universe, the apex point has been identified with God (see Chapter 6). This point is exactly at 0.7500 and must be maintained to continue the Universe. As the origin or source, this point represents the geometrical functional location of God in the Universe.

If the ultimate Deity is identified with the apex point of the Universe, then there must be a special significance that can be attributed to the apex point of the Eaverse, the structure associated with Evil. Suitable names have already been called out in the various Religions. Evil has been denoted as being exclusively the domain of the God of darkness. His other names include "Satan" and "The Devil". Thus the critical point of 0.1875 in the Range of Evil represents the geometrical functional location of the Devil in the Eaverse.

This critical point of 0.1875 in the Range of Evil also represents the mathematical value of that which is called "Satan" or "The Devil." This critical point is the apex of the included mathematical structure whose associated geometry can also be likened to a pyramid. The comparable point in the developed structure of the Universe was shown to be the mathematical value of God (see Chapter 6). In similar fashion to the apex of Good (which is God), the apex of Evil can be identified with the Devil. Thus the derivation of the critical point (0.1875) of the Range of Evil also provides the mathematical value that is associated with the Devil.

Not only are the respective apex points the critical locations for the Universe (Good) and the Eaverse (Evil), they are totally isolated from each other. This means that God and the Devil are effectively separated from one another. Their powers can not be directly used against each other. The only location where the two sets of powers can be wielded against each other is where there is a match of the geometrical relationships of their numerical ranges. This common medium or place is in the Second Dimensional Group of the existent Universe. This location is also the repository for all the Souls of Mankind. There is also the extension of existence for Matter. Thus aspects of Life and Matter allow for the concurrent operations of both Good and Evil!

From the purely mathematical point of view, the Range of Good (the Universe) is exactly four (4) times greater than the Range of Evil (the Eaverse). The main implication here is that the domain of God is four times greater than the domain of the Devil. Using this relationship, it can further be concluded that the significance and the importance of God is more extensive than that of the Devil. Thus God takes on the special characteristic denoting that He is the supreme being.

Since the Universe and the Eaverse are separate from each other, there need not be any time synchronism with respect to the resulting happenings of their associated operations. Things that happen in one of these major locations need not have any corresponding event take place in the other location. This means that in addition to their separation geometrically, they are also separated in time. Thus there is relative independence between the Universe and the Eaverse, so that each may exist separately.

Due to the much smaller numerical values that are involved in the extent of the range of its being, the Eaverse had the capability to establish itself prior to the Creation of the Universe. Thus at the Moment of Creation (for the Universe), the Eaverse was already operational and functioning. The Creation of the Universe has already been mentioned as occurring under the major associated condition of Nothing. When the separate Eaverse is considered, the implication is that there was something available to facilitate and influence various aspects of the Creation of the Universe. It must be

273

remembered that the Eaverse is directly associated with the Concept of Evil. Especially important is the implication that a control mechanism is provided by the Eaverse for the Creation of the Universe from Nothing.

The possibility must now be considered that aspects of the Creation and the development of the Universe are actually referenced by Evil. If the Eaverse does provide a control mechanism, then this implication becomes a most distinct possibility. But this raises a very critical point of argumentation. It has been stated (see Chapter 14) that the main Theological reason for the Creation of the Universe was to allow for the manifestation of the thinking process of God. If the implementation of this process is facilitated by the Eaverse and its association with Evil, this appears to be in direct contradistinction to the necessary good characteristics associated with God. It is like saying that the Devil had a hand in the development of God and His Universe!

Thus it is seen that the Concept of Evil is extremely far-reaching. Its origin officially begins in its own structural system called the Eaverse. Its included mathematics as expressed in the numerical values of the Range of Evil, show that there are functional compatibilities with the Souls of Mankind and with the Matter of the Universe. Through these various items, Evil has the propensity to enter and then influence the operations and happenings in the Universe.

Evil may even have the capability of affecting and influencing God! It is Evil, through the operations in the Eaverse, that actually provides the initial referencing for the control of the processes involved in the Creation and the primary development of the Universe. Since it is the Universe that allows for the thinking process of God, Evil will actually reference some of this thinking. This is why it seems that God does not always act in a truly good manner. It also offers an explanation why Evil enters into the workings of that which should be inviolate good operations, such as those

274

usually associated with good people or good institutions including Religions.

Thus Evil has the capability and the propensity to affect and influence anything. Such is the extent and the power of Evil. It is a force and a process which can now be identified. With a direct knowledge of Evil, many of its affects can be nullified. Various disease and health problems can be approached using cancellation techniques referenced by the mathematics of Evil. Prayers can take on new meaning and produce more desired results if they are directed in their application to bypass effects of the Concept of Evil. Much suffering and sorrow could be reduced or eliminated by effectively countering the influence of aspects of Evil. Thus Evil is identified as an individual set of operations which must be understood and dealt with separately from those of the Universe.

28

LOVE AND HATE

"A time to love, and a time to hate;"
(The Bible, O.T., Ecclesiastes 3:8)

Using the symbolisms established in Theology, the Concepts of Love and Hate can be examined in the perspective of the relationship included within the general order of things in the totality of the Cosmos. The identification and the examination of Evil (see Chapter 27) has shown that, from both the actual and the symbolic points of view, it can be associated with a completely separate system that occupies a portion of the super structure of existence, that also includes the entire Universe within its huge framework. If this huge super structure of the Cosmos according to this investigation is now considered to include at least the two systems of the Universe and the Eaverse (where each is associated with the Concept of Good and Evil respectively), then it is possible that other systems of significant size and influence are also contained within the framework of the overall

276

Cosmos. It will now be shown that there are other such systems. Indeed, the next two systems of importance can be identified and associated symbolically with various aspects of the Concepts of Love and Hate.

The first clue to all this is the identifying of God with light. The origin of this comparison lies in the roots of Zoroastrianism. Here the good God (Ahura Mazda) was associated with light while the evil God (Ahriman) was associated with darkness. These ideas spread to many other Religions in both the west and the east. Christianity produced such statements in its Scriptures as "that God is light, and in him is no darkness at all" (The Bible, N.T., 1 John 1:5). "I am come a light into the world, that whosoever believeth on me should not abide in darkness" (The Bible, N.T., John 12:46). "To open their eyes, and to turn them from darkness to light, and from the power of Satan unto God" (The Bible, N.T., The Acts 26:18).

In addition to light, God is also associated with Love. The Scriptures of the various Religions make such reference as "God is love; and he that dwelleth in love dwelleth in God, and God in him" (The Bible, 1 John 4:16). THUS GOD IS SYMBOLIZED BY LIGHT AND ALSO BY LOVE.

The importance and connection of all this will soon be made clear by the use of one more quotation from Scriptures. From the Old Testament it is stated—

"And God saw the light, that it was good;"
(The Bible, O.T., Genesis 1:4)

This quotation was also used in Chapter 19 which involved the derivation of the speed of light. It was stated in this chapter that the end process of vision or eye-sight occurs within the FOURTH Group of dimensions. If light is associated with the FOURTH Group, then its counterpart of "Love" has a similar association.

Of the first four significant systems in the Cosmos, we have now identified them symbolically as (1) Good or the Universe, (2) Evil or the Eaverse, and (4) Love. Only No. 3 remains unidentified. Since only the Concept of Hate has not been accounted for, it can be associated with System No. 3.

It is fitting that "Hate" be identified with the Third System. In its symbolism, this places Hate right next to "Evil." Since there is a repeating of the sequence after the number "4," Love in the fourth position is followed by Good in the first position. Thus the Concepts of Good and Love are adjacent to each other.

An order is evolving out of this symbolism. With the Universe (good) considered as the main system, the order of the first four systems or concepts is

1. Good
2. Evil
3. Hate
4. Love

Since mathematical relationships have already been developed for the first two categories, it is now possible to derive pertinent information for the areas of Love and Hate as well.

The factor of four which was developed and noted in the derivation of Evil, will be used again. The mathematics of the geometry works on the quaternary based system (see the book of PHYSICS). This means that the base is four and the relationships will repeat on a cycle of fours.

It was shown that the mathematical Range of Evil is directly related to the Range of Good by a factor of four. By similarity, it can be shown that there are corresponding Ranges for the mathematical realms of both Hate and Love, and that these also will be in ordered sequence developed in ratios identifiable to the base four. When the associated relationships are developed, the results can be itemized for presentation as shown in Figure 8.

278

DIMENSIONAL GROUP	SYMBOL NAME	LOWER LIMIT	CENTER VALUE	UPPER LIMIT	UPPER – LOWER RANGE
1	Good (Universe)	.60000000	.75000000	1.00000000	.40000000
2	Evil (Eqverse)	.15000000	.18750000	.25000000	.10000000
3	Hate	.03750000	.04487500	.06250000	.02500000
4	Love	.00937500	.01171875	.01562500	.00625000
	TOTALS →	.79687500	.99609375	1.32812500	.53125000
	TO LIMIT →	.80000000	1.00000000	1.33333333	.53333333
	FRACTIONS →	$\frac{4}{5}$	$\frac{4}{4}$	$\frac{4}{3}$	$\frac{8}{15} = \frac{4}{5} \times \frac{4}{3}$

FIGURE 8 – TABULATION OF THE FIRST FOUR SYSTEMS OF THE COSMOS

Figure 8 shows the Tabulation of the First Four Systems of the Cosmos. These include Good, Evil, Hate, and Love which are symbolically depicted and associated with the Dimensional Groups 1, 2, 3, and 4 respectively. The various mathematical values for each of the upper and lower limits are presented along with the geometric-mean center values. The extent of each range is also listed. This range value is obtained by subtracting the Lower from the Upper Limit in each case. For further examination and comparison, each column is totalled and then taken to the final mathematical limit that would occur if an infinite series was present in each column. The fractional value of each limit has also been noted.

The center values of each range are of special interest since they represent the geometrical mean of each range. As such, they denote the symbolic connotation that is associated with each range. For the Range of Good, the 3/4 center value represents God. For the Range of Evil, the 3/16 center value represents the Devil or Satan. This interpretation could be continued, so that for a Polytheistic Theological determination, each of the respective Gods would have an included mathematical value. This would provide for a complete set of Deities with a Supreme God in the dominant mathematical position.

By the use of the concepts described within this chapter, a full mathematical derivation can be made for any Monotheistic or Polytheistic Theological System. This means that a specific mathematical value can be developed for any Deity in any religious system, once the order of the relative significance of each God is known. Each pair of adjacent Gods in the known structured order bears a quaternary relationship to each other. The considered more significant Deity of the pair will have a mathematical value that is exactly four times that of the other.

What has been evolving in this chapter is the development

of a structured relationship system with a quaternary base. The specifically cited quaternary has been the symbolic representation of Good, Evil, Hate, and Love. Each of these has an associated mathematical equivalent value which has been noted in the "Center Value" Column shown on Figure 8. In turn, each of these noted decimal values can be replaced by an equivalent fraction. Since the symbolism of these values denotes an ordered function, the various individual representations of each form a series structure when they are considered in their totality. The sum limit of this series function is equal to one (1). This series function can be expressed in generalized mathematical form as follows:

$$f(x) = 3/4 + 3/16 + 3/64 + 3/256 + \text{---} + 3/4^n + \text{---}$$
$$= 3\,[1/4 + 1/16 + 1/64 + 1/256 + \text{---} + 1/4^n + \text{---}]$$
$$= 3\,[1/3]$$
$$= 1$$

The sum of the quaternary series approaches 1/3 as "n" approaches infinity (∞). The value "3" indicates that each dimensional GROUP "n" consists of 3 sets of dimensions. Thus from a geometrical point of view, we have a series mathematical function with an infinite number of parts whose sum total adds up to the value of one (1) or 100%.

What all this means is this. The Concept of Evil has led to the conclusion that there is an independent structure which is separate from that of the Universe. The Concepts of Love and Hate indicate that each of these can be identified with other independent structures located within the overall Cosmos, which are also separate from the Universe as well as being separate from each other. Thus with the Universe (which can be said to symbolize Good), we now have four separate systems or structures which together account for over 99.6% of the total Cosmos (see Figure 8).

These four separate structures have a number of other

meanings and can be used to provide many further interpretations in a wide variety of subject areas. In addition to symbolizing the Concepts of Good, Evil, Hate, and Love, the overall aspects of these developments can be used to represent numerous other things. This implicational possibility was the major reason for using and stressing the word "symbolize".

From a mathematical point of view, the Center Values (see Figure 8) of these four systems of the Cosmos provide the first four terms of an infinite series (see the previous equations for $f(x) = 1$). The sum of all the terms of this infinite mathematical series is equal to one. Thus we have a mathematical expression that can be used to define the aspects of the value of one.

From a geometrical point of view, the infinite series can also be used to express the portions of a multi-dimensional geometry. This multi-dimensional geometry can provide the mathematical definition for describing the container of the Universe, as well as those of the other structures of the Cosmos.

Many concepts and relationships can be explained using this quaternary based mathematical series. Since the significant geometry of the Universe exactly follows (in reverse form) this infinite series in its growth and development, all things within the Universe will follow its included ratios as well. The Concepts of Good, Evil, Hate, and Love have already been shown to directly bear out and use the cited mathematical values. Thus it is that these relations can be said to hold in all the structures that are included in the overall Cosmos.

Especially the Concepts of Good, Evil, Hate, and Love apply to many aspects of Life as well as to Theology Theory. These basic four qualities provide the referencing to the many behavioral operations of both God and Man. With

282

these four important characteristics referenced in turn by mathematics, a highly detailed accounting can be made to provide for advanced examinations into many fields of study.

Thus it is that Love and Hate go well beyond their immediate implications to offer and provide capability for dealing with Theology and other subject areas. They form a special conjugate pair that relate to the previous other conjugate pair of Good and Evil in important ways. Each member of its respective pair is the exact opposite of its other member. In addition, there is a further relationship that can be noted between similar members of *both* of these conjugate pairs. Up to now in our discussions concerning the infinite mathematical series, only *addition* of the terms was considered. When the process of addition is used to examine various combinations of the included terms, one result that is obtained is called the "arithmetic mean." When the process of *multiplication* is used, then a "geometric mean" can be obtained.

In the first portion of the infinite series beginning with the quaternary Good (.75000000), Evil (.18750000), Hate (.04687500), and Love (.01171875), the similar two outer terms (Good and Love) can be multiplied by each other and that result will be the same as the product of the two similar inner terms (Evil and Hate).

GEOMETRIC MEAN RELATIONSHIP

Good × Love =
.75000000 × .01171875 = .0087890625

Evil × Hate =
.18750000 × .04687500 = .0087890625

Thus: Good × Love = Evil × Hate

283

Good, Evil, Hate, and Love can be represented by dimensional groups 1, 2, 3 and 4 respectively. Thus in each separate such quaternary, the product of the associated positions of 1 × 4 will equal 2 × 3.

Although the depicted order of Good, Evil, Hate, and Love has been presented as shown, the actual order is in the reverse form. With Creation, the geometry starts with extremely small values. These increase in each term of the numerical sequence until the last term is finally reached. This last term is symbolized by the Concept of Good. The final four terms of this huge sequence are actually Love, Hate, Evil, and Good which are really developed in this order as shown. Thus the Concept of Love comes first before the development of the other major aspects.

The symbolism of Love coming first is especially noteworthy. The various Religions have all contended that Love is paramount and that Love comes first before anything else. With Love in the primary position, then all following things can be said to be referenced by Love. Thus the aesthetic is served as well as the practical.

Next in the general order is Hate, the very antithesis of Love. Since every succeeding something is greater than its predecessor, Hate is seen as being numerically greater than Love. Hate leads most naturally into Evil, the next aspect of the general order. But Evil, in turn, must give way to Good, the ultimate thing in the general order of things. This is consistent with the precepts of Theology where Good is considered to be the finest and the final purpose.

Thus Love is the gateway to God. But the path also lies through Hate and Evil. All these must be dealt with, if the ultimate Good is to be achieved. This is the quaternary of Love, Hate, Evil, and Good. The beginning must traverse through Love and Hate.

It is the symbolism of Love, Hate, Evil, and Good that offers the most important utility value of this composite concept. This quaternary presents the numerically most significant terms of an entire infinite mathematical series whose summation adds up exactly to the value of one (1). This series provides the mathematical key to the geometry and the major operations of the Cosmos as well as the Universe. Thus the Theological Quaternary of Love, Hate, Evil, and Good, provides the utility symbolism that can be used to reference everything else!

29

GOD AND TIME

*"To every thing there is a season, and a time to
every purpose under the heaven."*
(The Bible, O.T., Ecclesiastes 3:1)

Time forms a very special relationship with God. During
the various discussions of Theology, aspects of Time have
come up again and again. Time has appeared in many of the
different descriptions as a very necessary ingredient. Even
more, Time has referenced many of the explanations. Indeed, it will be seen that God and Time are inter-dependent
upon each other and have a number of very important aspects in common.

Of all the many subjects included within Science, Philosophy, and Theology, the Concept of Time is perhaps the most
unusual and the most important because of its unique capability to deal with everything and explain anything. Anything can be related to anything else and explained in terms
of Time. Time is a definite candidate for being chosen the
universal means for problem solving. In one of its more

usual aspects, Time represents rates of change and offers itself as a measure of such change. Change is what any something may do as a result of being a part of some happening or interaction. But in its priority aspect, Time must be considered as the initiator of change. It is Time that actually references everything. Doing this, Time becomes the priority entity in the Universe. It provides for the necessary means to

1. Initiate each and every function and operation.
2. Put these into groups and sequences as required.
3. Synchronize, separate, or delay as may be required.

It is within these capabilities to mark change and to reference everything that we now examine God in His various relationships that involve Time. Let us begin with some of the facts that have been brought out herein concerning the Time Aspects of Theology which are related to the existent Universe:

1. That which is known as the Universe, operates on a repeating cyclical basis (see Chapter 23).
2. The Time for one complete cycle of the Universe is 24 billion years. In Alpha-Omega Time representation, Omega equals 24 billion years (see Chapter 20).
3. There are prescribed definite mathematical proportions or ratios related to this Cycle which involve the happening of major events in the Universe (see Chapter 10).
4. Included among the priority proportions are the ratios 1/8 (Sex Point or Thinking Point), 1/2 (Wisdom Point), and 7/8 (beginning of Termination or the Termination Phase Point).
5. The Geological age of the Earth has been noted as being 4 billion years old (see Chapter 20).
6. The creation of the Earth took place at approximately 8

billion years into the cycle of the Universe, or when the Universe was 8 billion years old.

7. The Earth is scheduled to terminate at the end of its natural cycle (unless ended sooner because of catastrophic reasons) when the Universe is 16 billion years old (see Chapter 26).

8. Both Genesis 1 (The Bible) and the Creation Hymn X:129 (Rig Veda of Hinduism) are estimated to have been written approximately 4,000 years ago (see Chapter 2).

9. Genesis 1 (The Bible) depicts the creation of the Earth as it happened approximately 4 billion years ago at a time when the Universe was already 8 billion years old.

10. The Creation of the Universe was marked by the first thing created (The Creation of the phenomenon of God) which happened approximately 12 billion years ago. In Alpha-Omega Time representation, Alpha equals 0 (see Chapters 6 and 20).

11. At the Initial Creation, the Universe had no developed environment nor any of the necessary conditions to empower God with the capabilities of a thinking process. Therefore, the operations associated with the Creation of the Universe could not possibly have been under the knowing control of God.

12. The environment and the conditions of the Universe necessary to support useful thinking by God became available after the first 3 billion years into the existence cycle of the Universe.

13. When the Earth was created at 8 billion years into the existence cycle of the Universe, the thinking capabilities of God were in operation and had become highly developed.

14. Binary mathematical relationships involving halving and doubling have been disclosed in functionings of the existent Universe (see Chapter 23).

15. At the half-way mark (Wisdom Point), the geometry of

the multi-dimensions of the Universe doubled and developed into the final group of dimensions, which became known as the conventional or Euclidean 3-dimensional group (or Group 1).

16. At this same half-way mark (Wisdom Point), which occurred 12 billion years into the Universe's existence cycle, the Wisdom Point in the thinking capability of God was reached.

17. At this same half-way mark (Wisdom Point), on Earth where the Geological age was becoming 4 billion years, the wisdom point for Man was also reached.

18. At this same half-way mark (Wisdom Point), God obtained His capability for wisdom through the gaining of wisdom by Man, who is at the extreme end limit of the overall structure of the entire system of Life (see Chapter 25).

19. At the Universe age of 16 billion years, when the Earth is scheduled for natural termination, God is operating with full capabilities for wisdom.

20. At the Universe age of 21 billion years when the natural Termination of the Universe begins, the period marked by the wisdom of God ends due to the deterioration of the environment and the associated conditions within the universe that are necessary to support thinking.

21. From 21 to 24 billion years of age (referred to the existence cycle of the Universe), the Universe and the manifestation of God reverse their related development operations and proceed back to the minimal situation at Initial Creation.

22. During this Termination period, useful thinking is not possible. Once again, operations in the Universe proceed by DEFINITION and NOT by outside thinking control.

23. Finally at the age of approximately 24 billion years, the Universe and the existent Presence (phenomenon manifestation) of God both Terminate.

24. After Termination, identification of God is only with the noumenon or the Soul of God that is located in the Realm of Nothing.

Within the existent Universe, aspects of "age" have been noted continually. We have considered the age of the Universe, the age of the Earth, and the age of Man. This concept of age and aging is something that is only associated with the existent Universe. Aging involves change, and change can only take place in existence. The measure of aging (which is usually given in years) relates to the associated measure of change in some particular aspect of existence. When there is no existence, there can be no aging.

Aging, when measured in some term like years, can be related to Time. Since the process of aging occurs in the existent Universe, the EFFECTS of Time can only be manifested in the existent Universe. The effects of Time represent what Time DOES, so that these can be called the phenomena of Time. Thus Time, similar to God, is represented as a phenomenon in the existent Universe.

But Time is a concept that involves a simultaneous duality. In addition to its operation in the existent Universe, aspects of Time can also be identified within the Realm of Nothing. Since there is nothing within the Realm of Nothing, there is nothing to age or change. Therefore, no phenomenon of Time is possible within the Realm of Nothing.

It is the noumenon of Time which can be identified as being located within the Realm of Nothing. Time is the Scientific and the Mechanistic reference of everything and anything that happens anywhere in any Realm. Such a reference must be independent of any transitions or changes that can occur in the existent Universe. The Noumenon of Time must always be available to perform its referencing function. This availability requirement precludes its identification with the Universe, since this realm undergoes cycles of existence between which there is interruption in the continuity. The only location of relative stability, where there is never any interruption, is the Realm of Nothing. Therefore, the reference or Noumenon of Time is identified with the Realm of Nothing. But there is something else of tremendous significance also located in this Realm of Nothing. The Soul of God has also been identified in the Realm of Nothing. The Soul of God is the reference of the Deity and all Theology, and indeed is the reference of everything that comes about in the Universe. From the Scientific or strictly technical point of view, the Noumenon of Time is also the reference of everything that can or ever will be in the Universe. From this comes the conclusion that there must be a merging of the references of Theology and of Technology.

The Noumenon of Time is identified with the Soul of God to provide the means of initiating and implementing all functions and operations of the Universe, including those of God. Thus God and Time are considered to be one and the same entity. The concept of God provides for the Theology of the Universe. But it is the concept of Time that provides for the practical implementation of His will and His work.

30

THE NEXT BEGINNING

"According to the grace of God which is given
unto me, as a wise masterbuilder, I have laid
the foundation, and another buildeth thereon.
But let every man take heed how he buildeth
thereupon."
(The Bible, N.T., 1 Corinthians 3:10)

Thus was it before, and thus will it be again. For anything is what it is by virtue of its meeting the definition of its own existence. So states the primary concept of existence as presented in the book of EXISTENCE. And so it is that the prelude is set up for the beginning of the next Creation of the Universe.

The existent Universe, as a cyclical entity, has the inherent propensity to repeat itself in a specific ordered sequence pattern extending from Initial Creation to Final Termination. This capability to cyclically repeat is in accordance with the attendant characteristics of Existence Theory. For given the same circumstances and the same associated conditions, the consequences, events, and operational results must always be the same.

It has happened before, and it will happen again. And

292

again. And again. And again. For such is the unalterable arrangement of existence. And such is the pattern for the operations and the functioning of the existent Universe.

This pattern for the operations of the existent Universe can be precisely defined in terms of the Equations of Existence and the associated E-L-M Tabulations (see the book of EXISTENCE). These mathematically develop the arrangement and content of the various Steps that take place in the progressing operations and happenings that occur in the existent Universe between its Creation and its ultimate Termination. The overall order of these sequential Steps is absolute and predestined by definition, and will repeat in the exact manner for each and every cycle of the recurring Universe.

It should be noted that associated with each step are a number of points which represent events and conditions, of which all must be fulfilled prior to moving on to the next step. Although the order of the sequential steps is absolute, the order of the points is not this strict in requirement. The operations associated with the points between any two adjacent steps can be completed in almost any order, so that here a "free will" of choice can be exercised. Thus the concept of Predestination is associated with the Steps of Existence, while the concept known as Free Will is associated with the Points or the activities that take place between the Steps.

The proclamation of the Creation Hymn of the Hindu Vedantic Scriptures (see Chapter 2) is borne out when it proposes the possibility that the Universe actually was "MADE BY ITSELF." Indeed, these Scriptures represent a voice from ancient times shouting and begging to be heard from across a span of over 4,000 years ago. The power and the capability of the Scriptures of this as well as all the other major Religions, are far greater than has ever been suspected by the truly devout and the very faithful.

The definite predictable order and included functioning of

the operational steps, which provide for the existent presence of the Universe, is predestined and can be described by the specific definition developed by the associated mathematical pattern of existence. So definite is this pattern, that it can also be considered in terms of Time for its initiation, development, and maintenance. These time aspects are so important that one of the featured premises of Zen Buddhism involves special meditation (dhyana) where the attempt is made through prajna (the highest form of intuition) to actually cause the mind of the subject devotee to synchronize itself as fully as possible with these basic governing timing relationships that reference the operations of the Universe. Thus Existence Theory and Time Theory are necessary to Theology to provide and reference being and its included operations.

Although concepts of Existence and Time provide for the scientific aspects of the Universe, we must eventually turn to the ultimate Being, the reference of everything, for those concepts dealing with reason, meaning, and purpose. For it is God that references the Universe, taking priority over its existence and its operations.

The powers of God have been shown to be limited to just the two sets of operations that are identified with the general categories of Initiation and Termination. It can be said that it is God who is responsible for the Creation of the Universe. It is also God who can be said to be responsible for the final Termination of the Universe. Under certain circumstances, the cycle of the Universe need not go to its ultimate natural conclusion. Indeed, it can be prematurely Terminated at any time, thereby producing a catastrophic conclusion. This is well within the Termination power of God which can be exercised any time during the existence cycle after Creation.

Between each Initiation and Termination, no matter on what they are exercised, God can have no other power over the included subject operation, entity, or happening. The control of all the intermediate functionings always remains under the direct and sole influence of what is defined by Existence Theory. Things will be as they will be, in accordance with their own definition. Even God Himself must follow this mandatory requirement for existence, which is stated in the Holy Bible as—"I AM THAT I AM" (Exodus 3:14). Thus it is the Concept of Existence, and not God, that dictates and predetermines HOW everything must be for as long as it is said to exist.

But upon Termination, everything must cease to be. After Termination of the Universe, there will be the propensity to stabilize back into the steady-state condition that is characteristic of the emptiness or non-existence of the Realm of Nothing. Everything that existed before will be gone. The slate of the Universe will be wiped clean. All will be nothing. This is the same exact situation that was before the previous Creation.

Just as it was before, so will it be again. The same situation and conditions that were present prior to the last Creation will once again be prevailing.

At this time, only the non-existent Realm of Nothing is available. There is an absence of any kind of "container" which precludes the possibility of any dimensions. Without any container, there is no holding geometry, so there can be no existence of any kind. Thus there is nothing.

The only identifiable something within this Realm of Nothing is the Noumenon of Time and the Soul of God. These two entities form a conjugate pair, of which each has been shown to be synonymous with the other. This conjugate duality of the Noumenon of Time with the Soul of God represents the basic foundation and the totality of reference for everything that ever was, is, or ever will be.

From this duality of reference, everything else must follow. With the same conditions established that were identical to those previously encountered, the stage is set for a new

Beginning. Thus Creation can once again be Initiated, and with it, a new existent Universe can come into being. All shall be as it was before.

Behind everything, now and forever, is the conjugate duality of the Noumenon of Time with its synonymous relationship involving the operational aspects, personification, and the identification with the Soul of God. With this conjugate duality as the basic reference, everything else must result accordingly. These resulting effects will occur in orderly fashion by definition, and then will be said to exist. Thus all being will initiate from this dual reference of Time and God.

Through the study and understanding of Time, all technology can eventually be known. But through God, all that can ever be said to exist, will find meaningful expression in the identification, perspective, and purpose of that very Being along with its associated Universe of existence.

INDEX OF SUBJECTS

absences, 38, 70
age of Earth, 202-204, 288, 290
age of Universe, 179, 181, 192-205, 203, 288
aging, 290
Ahriman, 29, 261, 277
Ahura Mazda, 29, 261, 271, 277
Allah, 29
alpha, 165-167, 248, 287, 288
animals, 26, 27
Animism, 27
Archeology, 44
Aristotle, 193, 194
Arithmetic Mean, 283
Astronomy, 65, 193, 198
Atheism, 245
atom, 66
atomic energy, 66
avatar, 29, 160, 238
Ayat (a Verse in the Koran)
   see Koran in Index of Scriptures

Beginning, 25-34, 220, 227
behavior patterns, 109, 123, 132, 282
Bible, 36, 37, 44, 46, 50, 75, 130, 138, 159, 165, 184, 217, 238, 288

Bible Number, 179, 184-191,
binary pattern, 232, 247, 288
biological structure, 164
Biology, 62, 178
Botany, 56
Brahma, 87, 89, 221
brain, 62-65, 85-90, 96, 120, 127, 164
Buddha, 159, 193
Buddhahood, 159
Buddhism, 29, 193, 194, 216, 221, 261

carry over functions, 102, 123, 130
Catholicism, 260
Center of Thinking, 63, 64, 139
center point, 140
center value, 280-282
Central Processing Unit (CPU), 91, 127
ceremony, 31
change, 28, 80, 83, 109, 122, 171, 174, 185, 211, 224, 287
chemicals, 64
Ching, 28
Christianity, 27, 29, 36, 37, 50, 137, 159, 160, 193, 194, 216, 238, 239, 261, 263, 267, 270

closed memory, 123, 128
closed system, 118, 119, 122, 131
coffee example, 119, 243
common medium, 64
computer, 91, 125, 127
conditions, 103, 190, 221, 230, 240, 242, 251, 288
Confucianism, 29, 194, 216
Confucius, 193
conjugate pair, 103, 104, 107, 111, 116, 133, 283, 295, 296
container of the Universe, 146-149, 157, 212, 216, 220, 222, 282, 295
continuity, 100-103, 110, 140, 141, 223
Continuity Concept of God, 223, 241
continuum, 105
contrast, 29, 51
control memory, 128
Cosmos, 162, 259, 271, 276, 282
CPU—see Central Processing Unit
Creation, 52, 101, 109, 134, 139, 181, 262
Creation Hymn, 35-45, 87, 88, 288, 293
Curve of Existence, 83, 199
Curve of Pre-Existence, 83
cyclical, 135, 162, 171, 179, 181, 210, 211, 220, 227-235, 288

darkness, 29, 190, 262, 263
death, 38, 121, 122, 130, 131, 209
deciduous tree, 57
deity, 27
Déjà Vu, 240
demons, 27, 262
destination, 107, 108
Devil, 29, 262, 268, 272-274, 280
dhyana, 294

digital computer example, 125-128
dimensional groups, 86, 99, 104, 117-123, 127, 128, 148, 179, 213
dimensions, 53, 54, 55, 56, 82, 86, 98, 148-152, 157, 179, 185, 289
discontinuity, 102
disembodied Soul, 121
disease, 128-131, 275
displacement effects, 171, 210
distance, 204, 205
Distribution of Existence, 55-67, 117-121, 129, 131
disturbances, 83, 102
Divine Destination, 107
Divine Origin, 107
Domain of Nothing (or Zero)—see Realm of Nothing
domains, 102
dualism, 29, 138-140
dynamic, 81, 210, 211

E, 69, 78, 82, 232, 267
Earth, 29, 30, 138, 139, 201-205, 252-256, 261, 287, 288
Eaverse, 259, 271-275, 276
ego, 152
ego representation, 162
Egyptian Religion, 27
electricity, 63, 64
E-L-M Tabulations, 69, 70, 78, 82, 95, 98-100, 108, 153, 161, 187, 232, 264, 293
energy, 61-64, 69, 78, 82, 94, 96, 99, 108, 157, 161, 216, 232
English System, 188, 189
Equation of Existence, 77, 231, 281
Equation of Steps and Points, 91, 186, 232
ESAN, 259

Eschatology, 209-218, 220
Euclidean, 117-120, 128, 179, 204, 214, 289
events, 195, 236-241
Evil, 19, 29, 258-275, 276-285
evil spirits, 130
existence, 37, 46, 47, 100-103, 134, 135, 219-223, 296
Existence, Definition of, 229
Existence, Generalized Curve of, 198, 199, 201, 204
Existence Theory, 69, 101, 115, 117, 124, 132, 146, 161, 162, 187, 192, 210, 294
Existence Continuum, 105, 106
extension of God, 160, 166, 247
eye, 60, 61
eyesight, 178, 179, 190, 191, 277
fading of memory, 118, 132
FI, 212
FILO, 212
First Creation, 139-141
flower example, 248, 249
FO, 212
food, 59, 70, 71
fountainhead, 71, 77, 79, 104, 160, 178, 246
Free Will, 91, 95-98, 158, 162, 234, 236-241, 293
functions:
    f (0), 102, 196, 198
    f (1/8), 96-99, 106, 153-155, 196, 198, 254-257, 287
    f (1/6), 203, 255
    f (1/4), 75, 265-267
    f (1/3), 198, 200, 254-257
    f (1/2), 97-99, 106, 153-155, 196, 254-257, 287-289
    f (2/3), 255, 256
    f (3/4), 69, 70, 75, 98, 280
    f (π/4), 98

f (7/8), 98, 99, 153, 196, 254-257, 287
f (1), 196, 200, 281, 282
f (12), 184-191

Gayomart, 262, 263
Generalized Curve of Existence, 198, 199, 201, 204
geographical locations, 31
Geology, 193, 198, 252, 287
geometrical structure, 95
Geometrical Mean, 280, 283
geometry, 37, 61, 63, 72, 105, 115, 119, 127, 138, 140, 141, 146, 157, 185, 186, 212
glass, 64
going in—coming out, 65
Golden Age of Greece, 194
Good, 29, 137, 258-275, 276-285
Gospels, 230
gravity, 202

Happening of Events, 236-241
Hate, 276-285
health problems, 128-131, 275
Heaven, 137-141
higher life, 163, 164
Hindu, 14, 29, 40, 76, 87-89, 124, 159, 293
Hinduism, 28, 29, 50, 87, 159, 160, 194, 195, 215, 216, 221, 238, 261, 262, 288
Holy Presence, 243, 257
Holy Trinity, 238

inclusion effect, 129, 130
Identification of God, 102, 138, 223, 242-249, 250-257, 286-291
image, 59, 60, 178, 179
immortality, 38, 70-72, 100, 105, 110

implementation of God, 245
imprint, 117, 118, 123, 124, 131,
    132
India, 238, 239
initial conditions, 70, 72, 150, 242
Initial Creation, 37, 47, 51-53, 68-
    70, 75-79, 80, 84, 86, 87, 90,
    103-107, 110, 125, 288
initiating explanation, 182
Initiation, 48, 52, 109, 181, 198
input-output, 65, 126
instinct, 123, 132
intellect, 26, 139, 195
intelligible, 139
interactions in a common medium,
    64
interface, 168
intuition, 28, 294
Islam, 27, 29, 36, 50, 137, 195, 216,
    260, 261, 267, 270
Israel, 185

Jacob, 185
Jainism, 194
Jerusalem, 185
Jesus, 29, 159, 160, 185, 193, 230,
    231, 238, 239, 260, 263
Judaism, 27, 29, 36, 50, 137, 159,
    194, 216, 259, 261, 270
Judgment, 209, 215

Kant, Immanuel, 116
Karma, 124, 215
Koran, 50, 55
Kung-Fu-tse, 193

L, 69, 70, 78, 94, 157, 232, 268, 269
L-Tabulation, 69, 70, 94, 105, 106,
    166, 232
Lao-tse, 28, 193
life, 56, 68-71, 82, 88, 89, 100, 104,

105, 118-121, 131, 157-159,
    161, 164, 181, 182, 216
life force, 56, 117
Life Range, 78, 82, 106, 124, 166
LIFO, 212
light, 29, 44, 63, 64, 96, 98, 116,
    189, 204, 267, 277
light, speed of, 184-191, 200, 204,
    277
LO, 212
logic, 169-173
Lord's Prayer, 137
Love, 276-285
lower limit, 280

M, 69, 70, 157, 232, 268, 269
M-Range, 78, 82
maintenance, 67, 78, 172, 173
Man, 26, 30, 159, 163-167, 168-176,
    216, 217, 255, 256, 289
Manes, Mani, 262, 269, 271
Manicheism, 50, 260-263, 267, 271
Manifestation of God, 103, 105,
    134, 136, 138, 141, 152, 157,
    161, 167, 180, 216, 221, 251
mathematical, 78, 84, 105, 106,
    109, 153, 180, 185, 186, 193,
    195, 197
mathematical models, 69, 232
mathematical proportions, 153, 252
matter, 69, 70, 99, 157, 161
maturity, 153
Maya, 14
mechanism, 51, 63, 65, 99, 105,
    123, 158, 271, 290
meditation, 28, 159
memory, 40, 86, 118, 120, 123, 130-
    132, 179, 214-216
mental health problems, 131
Metric System, 188, 189
mirror, 61

300

Mithra, 262, 263
Moment of Birth, 118, 131
Moment of Conception, 118, 122-
   124, 128, 132, 214
Monotheism, 20, 29, 245, 261
Monotheistic Derivation, 280
moodiness, 130
Mount Olympus, 137
Muhammed, 30
multi-dimensions, 53, 67, 69, 86,
   97-99, 106, 117-120, 125, 127,
   149, 179, 251, 282
multiple personality, 130

n-dimension, 83
New Testament, 180, 230
Nirvana, 221
Noah, 109
non-existence, 37, 38, 101-103, 135
nothing, 81-83, 102, 223, 244
noumenon, 104, 105, 108, 115, 116,
   133, 139, 251
noumenon of God, 103, 110, 134,
   139, 166, 167, 223, 251
noumenon of Time, 83, 102, 103,
   110, 111, 135, 136, 182, 224,
   290, 291, 296
noumenon-phenomenon
   conjugate, 103, 110, 116, 133,
   134
N.T.—see New Testament

Old Testament, 36, 37, 43, 159,
   194, 217, 270, 277
omega, 165-167, 248, 287, 288
omission, 258
Omnipotent God, 93-111
open memory, 123, 128
open system, 118-123, 131
operations, 56, 149, 168, 169, 186,
   274

Ophthalmology, 60
optics, 59
origin of Life, 178-180
organizational characteristics, 168-
   176
O.T.—see Old Testament

Pantheism, 29, 245
Paradise, 137
parallel, 84
parameters, 108
pattern recognition, 97
patterns, 95, 97, 110, 228, 229, 235
personality, 117, 118, 128, 179, 180,
   214
Phase Out Point, 98, 153, 196
phenomenon, 25, 29, 103, 104, 107,
   108, 116, 134, 139, 222, 251
phenomenon of God, 52, 84, 138,
   139, 157, 161, 162, 167, 181,
   190, 215, 216, 221, 222, 243,
   250, 251, 288
phenomenon of Time, 103, 290
philosophy, 286
phonograph example, 125
photodiodes, 64
phototransistors, 64
physical presence, 56, 116, 117,
   118-121, 125-132, 167, 191,
   213, 214
Physics, 101, 136, 146, 149, 151,
   182, 193, 198
Pi (π), 98
plants, 56-59
Plato, 193, 194
points, 95, 153, 158, 185, 189, 195,
   196, 240, 293
Polytheism, 20, 29, 159, 245, 261
Polytheistic Derivation, 280
power, 94, 108, 109, 161
power of God, 108, 109, 294

prajna, 28, 294
prayers, 275
Predestination, 95-97, 107, 157,
    162, 231, 234, 236-241, 293
Pre-Existence, 37, 83
pre-existent material, 38
Primordial Universe, 88
prior existence, 235
priority, 150, 159, 172, 173, 195,
    243, 252, 287, 294
Process, God as a 243, 249
prophecy, 231
Prophet, 30
psycho, 130
psychosomatic, 130
purpose, 26, 101, 107, 108, 173,
    231, 249
Purusha, 75

quaternary, 20, 278, 280-285
quaternary sum, 281
questions, 15, 16, 32, 33, 189, 191,
    227, 237, 258
quintessence, 16

Ra, 27
raison d'être, 180
RAM—see Random Access
    Memory
Random Access Memory, 127
ratio, 60, 61, 147, 153, 196, 198
ratio, substance-to-container, 146,
    147
Re, 27
reaction in a common medium, 64
Read Only Memory, 127
Realm of Nothing (or Zero), 46-
    49, 51, 52, 72, 82, 83, 102, 133-
    136, 137-140, 150-153, 167,
    223, 224, 227, 244-246, 250,
    251, 290

Red Sea, 109
reference, referencing, 100, 101,
    104, 105, 121, 125, 131-135,
    141, 161, 174, 177-183, 192,
    211, 223, 224, 244, 251, 274,
    290, 294-296
registers, 92
Reincarnation Effect, 118
Religion, origin of word, 27
Resurrection, 209, 239
Rig Veda, 35, 36, 88, 288
rites, 31
ritual, 27, 31
ROM—see Read Only Memory
roots, 57, 59

S.—see Sura
Saints, 230
Satan, 29, 268, 272-274, 280
satori, 28
Science, 136, 149, 177-183, 192,
    290, 291
second memory, 118, 123
seed examples, 47, 244, 248
seeing, 60
self-actualization, 152
self-realization, 247
senses, 14, 26, 138, 139, 228
sensible, 14, 139
series, 20, 84, 153, 196, 197, 280,
    282
sex, 96
Sex Point, 97, 153, 154, 287
Shintoism, 29, 50, 194
Shiva, Siva, 238
sickness, 128, 129
Sig-Group, 99
silicon, 64
size, 148, 171, 179, 192-205
sky, 57
Socrates, 194

302

Sodom and Gomorrah, 109
somatic, 130
Soul, 104, 105, 115-132, 137, 160,
    179-182, 214, 215, 219, 221,
    222
Soul of God, 111, 133-136, 139,
    141, 167, 182, 223, 224, 244,
    251, 257, 291, 296
spirit, 27, 56, 117, 121-124, 128-
    132, 214, 215
Spiritual Presence, 100, 103, 105,
    107, 110
star, 65, 116
static, 81, 210, 211
Steady State Concept, 80-84, 86,
    90, 244
Step Function,185
steps, 78, 90, 91, 108, 158, 161, 170,
    181, 185, 186, 189, 293
Steps and Points, Concept of, 78,
    79, 154, 190, 232-235, 236-241
substance of the Universe, 146-
    148, 157
Sun, 65, 66, 201
Sura (a chapter in the Koran), 50,
    55
Synoptic Gospels, 230

Tao, 28
Taoism, 28, 216
Tao te Ching, 28
te, 28
temperature, 202
temporary insanity, 131
Termination, 18, 48, 49, 90, 98-101,
    109, 134, 135, 196, 198-200,
    209-218, 293, 294
Termination Point, 153, 287
That, 38, 39
Theological Presence, 134

Theological Quaternary, 280-284,
    285
Theological Reasons, 145-155, 156-
    162
Thinking Point, 153, 154
thinking process, 42, 85-92, 93, 96,
    97, 106, 107, 117, 125-130,
    139, 149-155, 156-159, 164,
    194, 211, 214-216, 240, 251,
    288
thought, 62-64, 86, 240, 241
Time, 20, 48, 82, 83, 102, 103, 109-
    111, 123, 124, 134, 135, 195-
    198, 224, 290, 294, 296
Time Concepts, 94, 109-111, 135,
    197
Time Points, 91, 123, 124, 131
Time Theory, 110, 115, 129, 132,
    146, 162, 169-172, 182, 192,
    195, 198, 235, 294
train examples, 120, 121, 150, 243
transistors, 64
tree example, 57
Trimurti, 238
Trinity, 238
Tri-Point Concept, 99, 153

Universe, 11, 13-16, 25, 26, 36, 84,
    94
    Age of, 192-205
    Creation of, 36, 39-41, 46, 50-54
    First Creation In, 68-72
    Main Reason For, 145-155
    Repeating Cyclical, 227-235
    Secondary Reasons For, 156-162
    Size of, 192-205
    Termination of, 209-218
    Upper Limit, 280
    Utility Value, 284

Variations, time-cyclical, 227-235

303

Vedantic Scriptures, 34, 36, 47, 293
Vishnu, 238

Wheel of Samsara, 209
wire, 63
Wisdom, 85-92, 97, 98, 106, 107,
   139, 151-155, 194-196, 211,
   251
Wisdom Point, 85-92, 98, 153, 196,
   197, 200, 201, 288, 289

Zarathustra, 194

Zen, 28
Zen Buddhist, 28, 159, 294
zero, 65, 82, 101, 102, 196
zero condition, 83
zero dimension, 82, 86, 110, 140
Zero, Realm of—see Realm of
   Nothing
zero Universe, 147, 245
Zoroaster, 194, 269
Zoroastrianism, 29, 50, 194, 216,
   260-262, 269, 271, 277

INDEX OF SCRIPTURES

THE BIBLE—Old Testament (O.T.)

Ecclesiastes 1:9, 227
Ecclesiastes 1:10, 236
Ecclesiastes 3:1, 286
Ecclesiastes 3:8, 276
Exodus 3:14, 40, 165, 242, 295
Genesis 1:1, 36, 43, 46, 50, 75, 138, 190, 255
Genesis 1:2, 43, 44, 190
Genesis 1:3-4, 43, 184, 190, 191, 267, 277
Genesis 1:5-8, 43, 44
Genesis 1:26-27, 159, 160
Genesis 3:5, 258
Genesis 3:17, 268
Isaiah 37:26, 25
Isaiah 40:21, 192
Isaiah 59:14, 209
Job 1:21, 109
Proverbs 4:7, 145
Proverbs 8:33, 177
Proverbs 25:2, 5
Psalms 88:12, 46

THE BIBLE—New Testament (N.T.)

The Acts 26:18, 277

Colossians 1:15, 104, 124, 180
Colossians 1:18, 68
1 Corinthians 2:7, 93
1 Corinthians 2:10, 133
1 Corinthians 2:12, 250
1 Corinthians 3:10, 292
1 Corinthians 12:7, 156
1 Corinthians 12:12, 168
James 1:17, 271
John 3:5, 115
John 6:64, 231
John 12:46, 277
1 John 1:5, 277
1 John 4:16, 277
Luke 2:42-46, 238
Luke 8:2, 130
Matthew 6:9, 137
Matthew 6:10, 160, 245
Revelation 22:13, 165, 212, 248
Romans 5:12, 263
Romans 6:17, 268
Romans 6:20, 268
Romans 7:18, 263
1 Timothy 4:15, 13

HINDU SCRIPTURES
Creation Hymn (Rig Veda X:129), 34, 35-45, 47, 52, 88, 293

Hymn of Man (Rig Veda X:90), 75

Kaivalya Upanishad 8:9-10, 80, 89

Katha Upanishad I:13, 85, 87, 104

Maitri Upanishad VI:17, 87

THE KORAN (QUR-AN)
Sura II. Ayat 29 (S.II.29), 50
Sura III. Ayat 44 (S.III.44), 55

Tao tê Ching, 219

Zoroastrian AVESTA, 163